The Psalms: Gateway to Prayer

The Psalms:
Gateway to Prayer

Jeanne Kun

Copyright © 2013 by The Word Among Us Press

The Word Among Us Press
7115 Guilford Drive
Frederick, Maryland 21704
www.wau.org

18 17 16 15 14   2 3 4 5 6

ISBN 978-1-59325-221-2

Cover and Text Design: David Crosson

Library of Congress Cataloging-in-Publication Data

Kun, Jeanne, 1951-
  The Psalms : gateway to prayer / Jeanne Kun.
      p. cm.
  ISBN 978-1-59325-221-2
  1. Bible. O.T. Psalms—Textbooks. 2. Bible. O.T. Psalms—Devotional use. I. Title.
  BS1430.55.K86 2013
  223'.206--dc23
                                          2012036168

Contents

Welcome to
The Word Among Us
Keys to the Bible

Have you ever lost your keys? Everyone seems to have at least one "lost keys" story to tell. Maybe you had to break a window of your house or wait for the auto club to let you into your car. Whatever you had to do probably cost you—in time, energy, money, or all three. Keys are definitely important items to have on hand!

The guides in The Word Among Us Keys to the Bible series are meant to provide you with a handy set of keys that can "unlock" the treasures of the Scriptures for you. Scripture is God's living word. Within its pages we meet the Lord. So as we study and meditate on Scripture and unlock its many treasures, we discover the riches it contains—and in the process, we grow in intimacy with God.

Since 1982, *The Word Among Us* magazine has helped Catholics develop a deeper relationship with the Lord through daily meditations that bring the Scriptures to life. More than ever, Catholics today desire to read and pray with the Scriptures, and many have begun to form small faith-sharing groups to explore the Bible together.

We designed the Keys to the Bible series after conducting a survey among our magazine readers to learn what they wanted in a Catholic Bible study. We found that they were looking for easy-to-understand, faith-filled materials that approach Scripture from a clearly Catholic perspective. Moreover, they wanted a Bible study that would show them how they could apply what they learn from Scripture to their everyday lives. They also asked for sessions that they could complete in an hour or two.

Our goal was to design a simple, easy-to-use Bible study guide that is also challenging and thought provoking. We hope that this guide fulfills those admittedly ambitious goals. We are confident, however, that taking the time to go through this guide—whether by yourself, with a friend, or in a small group—will be a worthwhile endeavor that will bear fruit in your life.

How to Use the Guides in This Series

The study guides in the Keys to the Bible series are divided into six sessions, each dealing with a particular aspect of the topic. Before starting the first session, take the time to read the introduction, which sets the stage for the sessions that follow.

Whether you use this guide for personal reflection and study, as part of a faith-sharing group, or as an aid in your prayer time, be sure to begin each session with prayer. Ask God to open his word to you and to speak to you personally. Read each Scripture passage slowly and carefully. Then, take as much time as you need to meditate on the passage and pursue any thoughts it brings to mind. When you are ready, move on to the accompanying commentary, which offers various insights into the text.

Two sets of questions are included in each session to help you "mine" the Scripture passage and discover its relevance to your life. Those under the heading "Understand!" focus on the text itself and help you grasp what it means. Occasionally a question allows for a variety of answers and is meant to help you explore the passage from several angles. "Grow!" questions are intended to elicit a personal response by helping you examine your life in light of the values and truths that you uncover through your study of the Scripture passage and its setting. Under the headings "Reflect!" and "Act!" we offer suggestions to help you respond concretely to the challenges posed by the passage.

Finally, pertinent quotations from the Fathers of the Church as well as insights from contemporary writers appear throughout each session. Coupled with relevant selections from the *Catechism of the Catholic Church* and information about the history, geography, and culture of first-century Palestine, these selections (called "In the Spotlight") add new layers of understanding and insight to your study.

As is true with any learning resource, you will benefit the most from this study by writing your answers to the questions in the spaces provided. The simple act of writing can help you formulate your thoughts more clearly—and will also give you a record of your reflections and spiritual growth that you can return to in the future to see how much God has accomplished in your life. End your reading or study with a prayer thanking God for what you have learned—and ask the Holy Spirit to guide you in living out the call you have been given as a Christian in the world today.

Although the Scripture passages to be studied and the related verses for your reflection are printed in full in each guide (from the New Revised Standard Version: Catholic Edition), you will find it helpful to have a Bible on hand for looking up other passages and cross-references or for comparing different translations.

The format of the guides in The Word Among Us Keys to the Bible series is especially well suited for use in small groups. Some recommendations and practical tips for using this guide in a Bible discussion group are offered on pages 114-117.

We hope that *The Psalms: Gateway to Prayer* will unlock the meaning of the prayers and hymns of ancient Israel for you and draw you into deeper prayer and communion with God. Through this study guide, may you come to know the power and pleasure of praying the psalms as you make them your own.

The Word Among Us Press

Introduction

Entering the Gateway to Prayer

For nearly three millennia—from the days of King David to our own era—men and women from diverse lands and cultures have been lifting their hearts to God by praying and singing the psalms of ancient Israel. Originally a sort of hymnal for public prayer and liturgical worship in the Temple built by David's son King Solomon, the Book of Psalms has also imbued Christian worship since the days of the early Church.

As a devout Jew, Jesus prayed the psalms frequently and occasionally cited verses from them in his public discourses and conversations and controversies with the Jewish elders and scribes (for example, Mark 12:10-11, 35-37; Luke 20:42-43). He and his disciples sang psalms during the Last Supper before leaving for the Mount of Olives (Matthew 26:30; Mark 14:26). Jesus even prayed portions of the psalms as he hung on the cross (Mark 15:34; Luke 23:46). St. Paul quoted from them throughout his letters and urged his fellow Christians to sing "psalms, hymns, and spiritual songs" (Colossians 3:16; cf. Ephesians 5:19). And as the faith spread, the early Fathers of the Church maintained love and reverence for the Jewish psalms. St. Augustine exclaimed, "O, in what accents I spoke to you, my God, when I read the Psalms of David, those faithful songs and sounds of devotion. . . . O how I was enkindled by them toward you" (*Confessions,* Book IX). Eventually, the Catholic Church incorporated the ancient psalms into its official prayer, the Liturgy of the Hours.

The psalms have been handwritten on papyrus scrolls and the parchment pages of illuminated manuscripts, typeset in books massproduced by printing presses, recorded on audio CDs, and digitized and delivered electronically on devices like iPods or smartphones. Yet, however they come to us, the psalms invite us to pray. Moreover, they teach us *how* to pray, for they give us a rich vocabulary. In the psalms we can proclaim to God our wonder at his greatness. We can confess to him our sins and failures and tell him of our ecstatic joys, our profound sorrows, our deepest needs, and our hidden fears. Indeed, from them we learn the language of prayer. In praying the psalms, we speak to God and God speaks to us. The Book of Psalms—also commonly known as the Psalter—is a gateway opening to us the path to prayer.

Ancient Israel's Hymnal

In Hebrew, the Book of Psalms is called *Tehillim,* "Praises," a title that indeed conveys the spirit and meaning of these songs. Even when expressing anguish and pain, the psalmists still affirm God's goodness and faithfulness and voice tremendous confidence in him.

The Psalter consists of 150 compositions or prayer-poems, most of which were intended to be sung or accompanied by music. The individual psalms were written or composed over a period of more than eight hundred years, from the rise of the Davidic monarchy (1000 B.C.) to the time of the Maccabees (167 B.C.). Thus, the Book of Psalms is not the work of one single poet or composer but, rather, a collection of prayers written at different times for varying purposes.

The psalms were gathered together by "editors" who divided the collection into five book units, in imitation of the *Torah,* the first five books of the Jewish Scriptures.

> Book 1: Psalms 1–41, an early compilation of Davidic hymns
> Book 2: Psalms 42–72, an anthology of hymns from the
> northern kingdom
> Book 3: Psalms 73–89, an assortment of songs from the
> Temple singers
> Book 4: Psalms 90–106, psalms from a royal collection
> Book 5: Psalms 107–150, a second and expanded Davidic
> royal compilation

Within these five books, there are some smaller groupings, among them the "Songs of Ascent" (Psalms 120–134) and the Hallel psalms (113–118, 145–150). *Hallel* comes from a Hebrew word meaning "to praise." Hallel psalms are hymns of praise that were sung on specific occasions. Each of the first four books ends with a doxology (Psalms 41:13; 72:18-19; 89:52; 106:48). All of Psalm 150 is a fitting finale to the fifth book and the Psalter as a whole.

Attributions of authorship and references to musical settings were added at the beginning of many psalms by editors. They also gave titles to some psalms in order to associate a particular psalm with a specific person or to point to or suggest a historical event or setting for which the psalm may have been composed.

Biblical tradition as well as later Jewish and early Christian tradition long considered David to be the chief author of the psalms, mainly because he is mentioned by name no less than eighty-one times in the Psalter. Seventy-three—almost half of the collection's 150 psalms—have headings that can be rendered as a "psalm *of* David" or "psalm *for* David." Some of these psalms may have been written by David, as the Scriptures testify that he was skilled in song: he was called to play music for Saul (1 Samuel 16:23), and he danced before the ark of the Lord with song (2 Samuel 6:5). But his chief accomplishments were to establish Jerusalem as his own city and locate the worship of the Lord there. Thus, it is likely that many psalms were collected under his name or given a title meaning "belonging to David" or "of the royal collection." In any case, the entire Book of Psalms traditionally came to be closely associated with King David, who has often been called "God's singer" and the "sweet psalmist of Israel."

Among the other seventy-seven psalms, editorial headings include "of Asaph," "of Korah," or "Solomon," "Moses," "Heman the Ezrahite," and "Etan the Ezrahite." These attributions do not necessarily mean that the psalm was written by the particular person, but that it comes from the collection under his name—in some cases, collected by him, or written by him, or just related to the office he held. Asaph was one of David's chief musicians (1 Chronicles 16:5), so the psalms "of Asaph" most likely mean psalms belonging to the Temple collection. Psalms "of the Sons of Korah" (42–49) formed the repertoire of this family of Temple singers.

Composed as songs to be sung, many psalms have notes regarding the melody. For example, a note at the beginning of Psalm 22 specifies that it is to be sung to a song entitled "The Deer of the Dawn"; Psalms 69 and 80 were to be sung to the tune "Lilies," which must have been familiar to the Israelites. Other psalms have notes about the instruments to be played in accompaniment: Psalms 4, 54, 55, 61, and 67 contain the reference "with stringed instruments"; Psalm 5, "for the flutes." Unfortunately, these melodies have been lost, so the Psalter has come down to us as a collection of prayers to be recited rather than as the hymnal of songs it originally was.

Editorial decisions also account for the numbering of the psalms. When the Hebrew psalms were translated into Greek, Psalms 9–10 were combined as one psalm. Thus, in Greek (and Latin) translations, all the psalms from Psalm 10 on are one number short. The familiar psalm beginning "The LORD is my shepherd" is number 22 in Greek and 23 in Hebrew. This "one number short" situation continues until the Hebrew Psalm 147, which is divided into Psalms 146 and 147 in Greek. Thus, there remain 150 psalms in both Hebrew and Greek collections! Most contemporary English translations follow the Hebrew numbering.

Variations are also noticeable in the verse numbering in different translations. The Hebrew Psalter gives verse numbers to the titles. Consequently, the reference to David and Bathsheba in the title of Psalm 51 is verses 1-2 and "Have mercy" begins verse 3. However, in many English translations, especially those associated with the New Revised Standard Version, the titles have no verse number. In these versions, "Have mercy" is verse 1 of Psalm 51. This study guide follows the NRSV (Catholic Edition). Understanding the differences in numbering will help avoid confusion when comparing different translations or when reading commentaries on the psalms.

Prayers for Every Mood and Occasion

The psalms have a universal appeal. The joyful shouts of praise and thanksgiving, the cries of distress, and the petitions and entreaties to God are all common responses arising out of the hearts of men and women everywhere. Who of us has not at some time or another echoed the groan "How long, O LORD? Will you forget me forever?" (Psalm 13:1) or reveled with gratitude in the goodness of God, singing, "I give you thanks, O LORD, with my whole heart" (Psalm 138:1)?

While joy, sorrow, praise, and lament are the most dominant themes pervading the entire Psalter, scholars recognize several major "types" of psalms and variously classify them according to content, structure, and life settings. The main classifications are wisdom psalms, hymns of praise, individual and collective laments, thanksgiving hymns, and royal and messianic psalms. Within these broad categories, several specific types are identifiable, among them penitential psalms, creation hymns, psalms recounting Israel's history, victory songs, and a royal wedding psalm. In some psalms, classifications or distinctions may overlap, blur, or run together.

Many of the psalms were probably composed as public liturgical prayers to be used in the Temple services in Jerusalem. Sometime after the fifth century B.C., the Jewish community also began to worship in local synagogues. The liturgy of the synagogues was a liturgy of the word that included readings from the Hebrew Scriptures and the singing of psalms. When Christian communities began to form, they imitated the worship of their Jewish brothers and sisters. Despite their public use, most of the psalms contain a very personal note, including strong emotions such as joy or anguish. Some may have begun as the personal private prayers of an individual and were later adapted for congregational use. As Pope Benedict XVI noted in a catechesis on the psalms,

> the whole complexity of human life is distilled in the complexity of the different literary forms of the various Psalms: hymns,

laments, individual entreaties and collective supplications, hymns of thanksgiving, penitential psalms, sapiential psalms and the other genres that are to be found in these poetic compositions. . . . By teaching us to pray, the Psalms teach us that even in desolation, even in sorrow, God's presence endures, it is a source of wonder and of solace; we can weep, implore, intercede, and complain, but in the awareness that we are walking toward the light, where praise can be definitive. As Psalm 36 teaches us: "with you is the fountain of life; in your light do we see light" (36:10). (General Audience, June 22, 2011)

The Christian Meaning of the Psalms

Our Jewish forefathers gave expression to their faith in God through the psalms and were gripped by a profound awareness of what it means to stand as mere creatures before the presence of God. As Christians, we have made their words our own, praying the psalms unchanged, for we have the same joy in the Lord, the same hope of deliverance, the same confidence in appealing to his mercy. However, we pray the psalms with an added richness because of our awareness of their fulfillment in Jesus Christ. They become more meaningful to us as we interpret them in light of the revelation of the new covenant.

The New Testament is the fulfillment of what is foreshadowed and prefigured in the Jewish Scriptures, known to Christians as the Old Testament. Recognizing this helps us to more easily understand and interpret both parts of the Bible. Many of the realities of the Old Testament are "types" of greater realities that are only fully revealed in the New Testament. The people, events, and institutions of the Old Testament have meaning in themselves, as parts of the unfolding of God's plan. But these same people, events, and institutions are also foreshadowings of people, events, and institutions that constitute the final unveiling of God's plan, his new covenant. In particular, many elements of the old covenant point the way to Jesus Christ, who is the new covenant.

The better we understand the old covenant and are able to interpret its types or shadows, the better we will be able to understand the new covenant. The psalms are one of the primary places in the Old Testament where we are able to see and understand the types in their original or immediate context and yet at the same time move beyond this immediate meaning to the greater spiritual reality they foreshadow.

A brief overview of God's action throughout salvation history helps clarify this idea and bring it into perspective. From the beginning, God's constant desire for mankind has been to unite us to himself as his sons and daughters. After the fall of Adam, God continued to work toward this purpose. He called Abraham to follow him and made Abraham our forefather in faith. God established a people and blessed them with a land of their own and a covenant, after delivering them by the leadership of Moses. God made them a priestly people who offered sacrifice to him, lived under the kingship of David, and awaited the day of the Lord and the coming of the Messiah. The psalms were written within the context of this salvation history and are full of references to all that identified Israel as a distinct people with a culture and heritage of their own—land, army, king, enemies, Temple worship, sacrifice, covenant, priesthood. These elements not only have meaning in themselves, but are also types of what was to come in the revelation brought by Jesus Christ. They foreshadowed greater truths. They are elements that make up the psalms and also elements that point beyond themselves.

With the incarnation of Jesus, his coming to us as the Word-made-flesh, we see the fulfillment of all that was foreshadowed in the Israel of old. Jesus is the new Adam. He is also the new Moses, the great high priest, and the anointed king or Messiah. Instead of having territorial land as in the era of the psalms, we, the new people of God, know our heritage as sons and daughters of God, and we know God's reign over the earth. Instead of fighting with physical armies against enemies, as on the battlefield of Israel, we victoriously pray the warrior's psalm (Psalm 144) as we engage in warfare against Satan and his hosts who are out to destroy God's people. The Temple is now present in the body of Christ, and Jesus is both high priest and holocaust. He has offered the greatest and perfect sacrifice for us on the cross. Ancient Zion foreshadowed the city of God, the new Jerusalem to come down from heaven. So it is with profound joy and anticipation that we exclaim, "I was glad when they said to me, / 'Let us go to the house of the LORD!' / Our feet are standing / within your gates, O Jerusalem!" (Psalm 122:1-2). It is there that we see Jesus, descended from David, enthroned as king forever (Psalm 110).

Thus, all the ancient types or prefigurements, full of meaning as they were in their original setting, are fully realized in the incarnation of Jesus and will be finally accomplished with his Second Coming. Interpreting the psalms with this awareness—grasping their prophetic content and the significance of the typology presented in them—makes it possible for us as Christians to pray them wholly unaltered from their original Hebrew form but with a new depth of meaning. Our voices repeat the words of the Israelites before us, yet the words now resound with a fullness that has come to us through our redemption in Jesus Christ.

Making the Psalms Our Own

By this Christian interpretation, we make the psalms our own and join with Christ in his own prayer. When we pray the psalms, whether alone or with fellow Christians, we participate in the prayer of the Church, God's people. We share the psalms in common as members of the body of Christ—in some of them, speaking the same prayers Christ himself offered to the Father; in others, hearing the Father's words addressed to us about his Son and acknowledging Jesus as our Lord.

Whether we pray the responsorial psalm in the daily Mass readings, pray the Divine Office, select a psalm randomly, or use some other format for incorporating the psalms into our time of prayer, we should try to pray all of them over a period of time. The repeated praying of psalms, whether or not it suits our mood or frame of mind at the moment, is what teaches us how to pray. The psalms give us a concrete experience of offering to God daily worship and praise. Just as the priestly people of Israel offered a sacrifice of praise and thanksgiving in the courts of the Lord (for example, Psalms 5:7; 66:13-15; 116:17-19; 118:19, 26), we, too, are servants of God offering this same sort of service of worship and sacrifice. And the psalms, inspired as they are by the Spirit of God and prayed by Jesus himself, can shape our own prayer and form our attitudes in practical Christian living.

For example, praying the penitential psalms can deepen our recognition of our human frailty and inclination to sin and, in addition, form our minds in the proper attitude to take before the Lord in repentance. An understanding of how to repent is instilled in us and is a great aid in times when we need to turn away from specific sins. Similarly, we can learn from the psalms responses of joy, praise, and gratitude to God for his constant goodness without relying on an emotional high to express them.

More important, however, than a proper technique or method with which to pray the palms is to simply give ourselves over to them, making them our own prayer that rises spontaneously and repeatedly to our lips and allowing them to take hold of our hearts. When we do so, we will discover that, as the well-known Trappist monk Thomas Merton wrote, "God will give Himself to us through the Psalter if we give ourselves to Him without reserve, in our recitation of the Psalms." And as Merton explained, this only requires "a pure faith and an intense desire of love and above all a firm hope of finding God hidden in His revealed word" (*Bread in the Wilderness*).

"Happy Are Those . . ."

Psalm 1:1-6

1 Happy are those
   who do not follow the advice of
     the wicked,
or take the path that sinners tread,
   or sit in the seat of scoffers;
2 but their delight is in the law of
     the LORD,
   and on his law they meditate day
     and night.
3 They are like trees
   planted by streams of water,
which yield their fruit in its season,
   and their leaves do not wither.
In all that they do, they prosper.

4 The wicked are not so,
   but are like chaff that the wind drives away.
5 Therefore the wicked will not stand in the judgment,
   nor sinners in the congregation of the righteous;
6 for the LORD watches over the way of the righteous,
   but the way of the wicked will perish.

> The collection of psalms found in Scripture, composed as it was under divine inspiration, has, from the very beginnings of the Church, shown a wonderful power of fostering devotion among Christians.
> —**Pope St. Pius X**

Psalm 119:1-8

1 Happy are those whose way is blameless,
   who walk in the law of the LORD.
2 Happy are those who keep his decrees,
   who seek him with their whole heart,
3 who also do no wrong,
   but walk in his ways.

⁴ You have commanded your precepts
    to be kept diligently.
⁵ O that my ways may be steadfast
    in keeping your statutes!
⁶ Then I shall not be put to shame,
    having my eyes fixed on all your commandments.
⁷ I will praise you with an upright heart,
    when I learn your righteous ordinances.
⁸ I will observe your statutes;
    do not utterly forsake me.

The Book of Psalms is a collection of sacred songs reflecting the prayers, praises, longings, laments, and aspirations that have moved the hearts of Jews and Christians in their communion with God for centuries. The collection grew by slow stages, over a period of eight hundred years of ancient Israel's history, and when it was "closed," the final form consisted of 150 psalms, as it does today. The psalm deliberately placed at the beginning of the collection serves as a "gateway," or preface, to the entire Book of Psalms. In fact, Psalm 1 may have been specifically composed for that purpose—to guide readers into the path that leads to a truly blessed and happy life.

Many psalms—among them, 1, 19, 37, 49, 78, 112, 119, 127, and 128—share the stylistic features and themes of the Wisdom literature of the Old Testament, which includes the books of Job, Proverbs, Song of Songs, Wisdom, Ecclesiastes, and Sirach. Wisdom literature frequently contrasts the virtues of the "righteous" (the just or good) and the vices of the "wicked" (the unjust or evil). It also extols the excellence of the divine "law of the Lord"—*Torah*, in Hebrew—and the benefits derived from adhering to it. Characteristically, its subject matter is instructive in tone and its composition formal.

It's notable that Psalm 1 opens with the expression "Happy (or blessed) are those," words that are found at least twenty-five more times throughout the psalms. These words are a beatitude that points to what a person needs to *avoid* as well as do in order to find happiness. The psalm's first verse anticipates Jesus' beatitudes (Matthew 5:1-11), which describe the "blessed" who belong to the kingdom of heaven and also serve as a preface to his entire Sermon on the Mount (5:1–7:29).

As a reflection on blessedness and righteousness, Psalm 1 is addressed to the reader rather than to God. Two ways are sharply contrasted: the path of the righteous who delight in keeping the law of the Lord and prosper and the path of the wicked who perish.

> Let's take our cue from Psalm 1, the gateway to the whole Book of Psalms, and meditate on the law of the Lord day and night.

The law of the Lord includes not only God's commandments but his "revelation," that is, the record of his acts of love to the people of Israel and the promises that he has communicated to them. Following the law is not burdensome but rather brings joy and delight to those who keep it (Psalm 1:2). Those who are righteous recognize the *Torah* as the standard by which they are to live. Psalm 119, perhaps the best known of the Wisdom psalms, beautifully illustrates with the force of repetition this theme introduced in Psalm 1.

They who are "happy" are compared to a tree, a symbol of prosperity and well-being. With roots reaching to streams of water, it flourishes and bears "fruit in its season" (Psalm 1:3). Most likely, this fruit means wisdom gained by good living and used for the benefit of others. Centuries later, Jesus used a similar illustration: "No good tree bears bad fruit, nor again does a bad tree bear good fruit; for each tree is known by its own fruit" (Luke 6:43-44).

The latter half of Psalm 1 describes the fate of those who ignore God's revelation and reject his love: The "wicked" are like "chaff that the wind drives away" (verse 4). In ancient Israel the winnowing process was used to thresh grain. First, the stalks of wheat were trod underfoot by oxen or people; then, this straw was thrown in the air over the threshing floor, which was usually a breezy mound. The heads of grain, loosened by the treading, fell to the floor and were gathered in, while the light, useless chaff was blown away by the wind. The psalmist's vivid imagery warns us against such a fate!

Let's take our cue from Psalm 1, the gateway to the whole Book of Psalms, and meditate on the law of the Lord day and night (verse 2), pondering God's revelation and instructions to us. As Cistercian monk and scholar M. Basil Pennington pointed out, "It is with the rich promise of the first Psalm, 'Blessed Are They,' that we enter the Psalter, knowing that the time we spend with it—be it during the quiet of the night or the pauses in the midst of the labors of the day—will be among the most fruitful of our lives" (*Psalms: A Spiritual Commentary*).

And as we read, pray, and reflect on the psalms that lie before us in this study, may we come to treasure the great riches we discover there!

Understand!

1. What negative practices do those who are "happy"—that is, the blessed righteous—avoid in Psalm 1:1? What positive actions and attitudes identify a just person?

_____

_____

_____

_____

_____

2. Note the verbs in the opening verse of Psalm 1. Describe in your own words how these verbs illustrate successive stages in moving away from the right path.

_____

_____

_____

_____

_____

3. Read Jeremiah 17:7-8 and compare the prophet's description with that of the psalmist in Psalm 1:3. What additional insights do you gain from Jeremiah? What can you learn from this image drawn from nature?

_____

_____

_____

_____

_____

4. What does Psalm 1 indicate about the condition and lot of those who do not follow God's way? What consequences do the "wicked" face?

_____

_____

_____

_____

_____

_____

5. What nouns does the psalmist use in Psalm 119:1-8 to variously describe God's law? How do these synonyms expand your understanding of _Torah_? What phrases describe the psalmist's attitude and response to God's law? In your opinion, is the technique of repetition effective in Psalm 119? Explain your answer.

_____

_____

_____

_____

_____

_____

▶ In the Spotlight
The Poetic Artistry of the Hebrew Psalms

The psalms are poems, but some of the original qualities of Hebrew poetry are not apparent when translated into other languages. For example, a technique of Hebrew poetry favored in the Wisdom literature and Wisdom psalms is the acrostic, or alphabetical, construction in which successive verses or groups of verses (stanzas or strophes) begin with the twenty-two successive letters of the Hebrew alphabet. This technique is highly developed in Psalm 119 and in the Book of Lamentations. Other examples of psalms that employ an acrostic structure are 9, 25, 34, 37, 111, and 145.

Parallelism is another dominant aspect of the beauty and nature of Hebrew poetry—and fortunately, parallelism comes through strongly even in translation and can be appreciated in any language. In this technique, the content of one line of the psalm is parallel to—that is, corresponds to—the content of another. (The verse-unit of two phrases is called a distich, and a unit of three lines is a tristich.)

Frequently the parallelism balances the same thought in a comparison that is highlighted by the repetition of the thought, as in the following examples from Psalm 96:6-8:

> Honor and majesty are before him;
> strength and beauty are in his sanctuary.

> Ascribe to the Lord, O families of the peoples,
> ascribe to the Lord glory and strength.
> Ascribe to the Lord the glory due his name.

Parallel balance may also be seen in a contrast of ideas or in two opposite thoughts: "in the morning [grass] flourishes and is renewed; / in the evening it fades and withers" (Psalm 90:6).

As you read the psalms throughout the course of this study, be alert to their wording and structure, and you will grow in your appreciation of their artistry as Hebrew poems.

Grow!

1. Whom do you associate with? Whom or what do you listen to? What do you look at? What choices are you frequently confronted with in your daily life? Recall an instance when you chose to act righteously in the face of temptation to go the "way of the wicked" (Psalm 1:6). In what ways did you experience the "happiness" of those who follow God's law?

_____

_____

_____

_____

_____

2. How often do you take time to meditate on the "law of the LORD" (Psalm 1:2)? What value do you find in this practice? What might you do to make reading and meditating on Scripture a more meaningful part of your life?

_____

_____

_____

_____

_____

3. Do you think your life corresponds to the psalmist's image of a tree planted by streams of water (Psalm 1:3)? Why or why not? What fruits are you bearing? How are others benefiting from this fruit?

_____

_____

_____

_____

_____

_____

4. What personal message does Psalm 1 hold for you? How can you
   put this message into practice in your life?

_____

_____

_____

_____

_____

5. Read Psalm 119:1-8 and ponder a few of the phrases found in it
   that describe God's law and our relationship to it. What is your
   response to this psalm? Do you "delight" in God's law or do you
   experience following God's ways as a burden that weighs you
   down? Explain your answer.

_____

_____

_____

_____

_____

▶ In the Spotlight
Psalm 119: A Launching Pad for Prayer

_Psalm 119 is the longest of the psalms. Its 176 verses are divided
into twenty-two strophes, or stanzas, of eight verses each. Each
strophe begins with a successive letter of the Hebrew alphabet
(which consists of twenty-two letters, from Aleph to Tau), and_

the first word of each of the strophe's eight verses begins with this same letter. Through continual repetition, the entire psalm highlights one theme: being rooted and anchored in the Torah— God's revelation, instructions, promises, words, and covenant.

Appreciation of this psalm [119] is a good test of one's understanding of the psalms as prayers. From the literary point of view, it does not reach a high level. It is monotonous, repetitious. . . . In short, the style is pedestrian, the construction mechanical, the thought-content unoriginal and meager.

And yet, rightly considered as a religious text, this is a great composition. It is intended to be a foundation or starting point for personal prayer. In this it corresponds somewhat to the Rosary, and its ABC has the function of our "beads." Deliberately, the same simple ideas and aspirations are repeated over and over, to help the mind of the one reciting it to concentrate on one thought, and to rouse his heart to aspirations of love. Individual verses, with their simple affirmation or urgent appeals, are not meant to be intellectually analyzed and studied (though, as a matter of fact, in their very simplicity they are rich in implications, and a whole theology could be constructed from this psalm). The author . . . undertook to build a launching pad, from which the devout soul might soar to loving contemplation of the unthinkable goodness of God. He knew what he meant to do, and he did it well.

—R.A.F. MacKenzie, SJ, *Old Testament Reading Guide*

Reflect!

1. Reflect on Psalm 1 as the gateway to the Book of Psalms. What do these descriptions tell you about the role and importance of this psalm? About the significance of the whole Book of Psalms? Keep these ideas in mind as you read and pray the psalms in this guide.

2. Reflect on the following Scripture passages that encourage us to walk in the way of the Lord and the path of the just:

> Moses summoned all Israel and said to them: . . . "See, I have set before you today life and prosperity, death and adversity. If you obey the commandments of the LORD your God that I am commanding you today, by loving the LORD your God, walking in his ways, and observing his commandments, decrees, and ordinances, then you shall live and become numerous, and the LORD your God will bless you in the land that you are entering to possess. But if your heart turns away and you do not hear, but are led astray to bow down to other gods and serve them, I declare to you today that you shall perish; you shall not live long in the land that you are crossing the Jordan to enter and possess. I call heaven and earth to witness against you today that I have set before you life and death, blessings and curses. Choose life so that you and your descendants may live, loving the LORD your God, obeying him, and holding fast to him; for that means life to you and length of days, so that you may live in the land that the LORD swore to give to your ancestors, to Abraham, to Isaac, and to Jacob." (Deuteronomy 29:2; 30:15-20)

> Do not enter the path of the wicked,
>   and do not walk in the way of evildoers.
> Avoid it; do not go on it;
>   turn away from it and pass on.
> For they cannot sleep unless they have done wrong;
>   they are robbed of sleep unless they have made
>   someone stumble.
> For they eat the bread of wickedness
>   and drink the wine of violence.
> But the path of the righteous is like the light of dawn,

which shines brighter and brighter until full day.
The way of the wicked is like deep darkness;
    they do not know what they stumble over.
(Proverbs 4:14-19)

The fear of the Lord is glory and exultation,
    and gladness and a crown of rejoicing.
The fear of the Lord delights the heart,
    and gives gladness and joy and long life.
Those who fear the Lord will have a happy end;
    on the day of their death they will be blessed.
(Sirach 1:11-13)

▶ In the Spotlight
The Power of the Hebrew Psalms

The following testimonies of two contemporary Jews, included by the renowned Jewish scholar Nahum M. Sarna in his study of the Book of Psalms entitled Songs of the Heart, *give striking witness to the power and impact of praying the psalms:*

A Jew from Yemen once told me how he celebrated his bar mitzvah back in the land of his birth. The family was desperately poor; there were no parties, no gifts, no excitement, no speeches. The boy simply went to the synagogue on the designated Sabbath morning and read the appropriate portion of the Torah with the traditional blessings before and after. But what left an indelible impression on him, the experience that continues to move him deeply even forty years later, was staying up all the previous night with his grandfather, and together reciting the entire Book of Psalms.

Anatoly Sharansky spent nearly nine terrible years of deprivation and suffering as a "prisoner of Zion" in Soviet prisons and labor camps. His "crime" consisted in wanting to leave the hell of the "workers' paradise" in order to migrate to the land of Israel. By his own testimony, during all the years of enforced isolation, oppressive loneliness, appalling misery, agonizing suffering, and unutterable anguish, it was the copy of the Hebrew Psalter that he kept with him that sustained his spirit, gave him the strength to endure his bitter fate, and imparted the courage to persevere in hope.

While he was incarcerated, his wife, Avital, accepted on his behalf an honorary Doctorate of Humane Letters from Yeshiva University in New York. On that occasion, she told the audience, "Anatoly has been educated to his Jewishness in a lonely cell in Chistopol prison where, locked alone with the Psalms of David, he found expression for his innermost feelings in the outpourings of the king of Israel thousands of years ago." When he was finally released, and arrived in Jerusalem, he was carried to the Western Wall by his friends and admirers still clasping in his hands his beloved Book of Psalms.

—**Nahum M. Sarna,** *Songs of the Heart*

Act!

Memorizing psalms is an ancient Christian custom. When we commit something to memory, we know it "by heart." Thus, we can spontaneously pray psalms that we have memorized as occasions and the events and needs of daily life move us, even when we don't have a Bible or Psalter at hand. As Rev. Ben Patterson advises,

Memorize the Psalms—but not by rote. Rather, learn them by heart; make their words your words. Come to understand them so well you can recite them—by inflection and tone—as though you had written them yourself. This is, by far, the best way I know to learn to pray the Psalms. I can think of no more powerful way to allow the Word of God to change who you are and how you think. Over the years I have been grateful for every line of Scripture I have committed to memory, but the prayers of the Psalms have offered incomparable comfort and clarity in desperate, murky, and confusing situations, when I didn't have a worthwhile word of my own to say—when I quite literally didn't have a prayer. (*God's Prayer Book*)

Choose a psalm, perhaps your favorite or one that speaks to a current need, and memorize it. During the coming week, pray this psalm from memory frequently so that its words truly become your own.

▶ In the Spotlight
A Psalm Is Delightful to Our Soul

All the books of Scripture, both Old Testament and New, are inspired by God and useful for instruction, as the Apostle says [2 Timothy 3:16]; but to those who really study it the Psalter yields especial treasure. . . . For I think that in the words of this book all human life is covered, with all its states and thoughts, and that nothing further can be found in man. For no matter what you seek, whether it be repentance and confession, or help in trouble and temptation or under persecution, whether you have been set free from plots and snares or, on the contrary, are sad for any reason, or whether, seeing yourself progressing and your enemy cast down, you want to praise and thank and bless the Lord, each of these things the Divine Psalms show you how to do, and in every case the words you want are written down for you, and you can say them as your own.

—**St. Athanasius of Alexandria,** *Letter to Marcellinus on the Interpretation of the Psalms*

In the same way that food is tasty, a psalm is delightful to the soul. It also needs to be chewed. If you swallow a psalm hastily in one gulp, you will miss the sweet taste. "They are sweeter than honey, than honey from the comb" (Psalm 19:10). Devotion can drip from the words of a psalm. "I will pray with my spirit, but I will also pray with my mind. I will sing with my spirit, but I will also sing with my mind" (1 Corinthians 14:15). Attentive devotion is imperative. It is not possible that those who are pleased with our earthly prayers will ignore us in heaven.

—**St. Bernard of Clairvaux,** *Talks on the Song of Songs*

"Make a Joyful Noise to the Lord"

Psalm 98:1-9

1 O sing to the LORD a new song,
    for he has done marvelous things.
His right hand and his holy arm
    have gotten him victory.
2 The LORD has made known his victory;
    he has revealed his vindication in the sight
        of the nations.
3 He has remembered his steadfast love
        and faithfulness
    to the house of Israel.
All the ends of the earth have seen
    the victory of our God.

4 Make a joyful noise to the LORD, all the
        earth;
    break forth into joyous song and sing praises.
5 Sing praises to the LORD with the lyre,
    with the lyre and the sound of melody.
6 With trumpets and the sound of the horn
    make a joyful noise before the King, the LORD.

7 Let the sea roar, and all that fills it;
    the world and those who live in it.
8 Let the floods clap their hands;
    let the hills sing together for joy
9 at the presence of the LORD, for he is coming
    to judge the earth.
He will judge the world with righteousness,
    and the peoples with equity.

The Lord's saving mercy reaches from one end of the earth to the other. Everyone and everything speaks to us of it by their very being. Everything calls forth from us the imperative: "Sing to the Lord a new song."
—M. Basil Pennington, OCSO

Scripture resounds with the worship of God. From its pages echo the voices of countless men and women—as well as myriads upon myriads of angels—who offer cries and prayers of homage to the Lord. We, too, can join this chorus of praise by making our own the words of those great hymns in the Book of Psalms that extol the Lord and his greatness.

The word "worship" is derived from the Old English *weorthscipe*— "to acknowledge the worth or value of something." Thus, when we worship God, we are recognizing and acclaiming his worth and rightly honoring him because of it. We worship God because of who he is—our Creator and Lord, the Holy One "worthy . . . to receive power and wealth and wisdom and might / and honor and glory and blessing!" (Revelation 5:12). We worship God because of the love, faithfulness, and mercy he continually shows us and because of his wondrous works. In fact, we have been created for this very purpose. And as we raise our voices to declare his praises, we can also raise our hearts to him—hearts filled with love and adoration.

Psalms that recount the praises of God in particular are called hymns and commonly open with a call or invitation to praise God. Often the psalmist addresses the summons to praise to himself, in the form of self-exhortation: "Bless the LORD, O my soul" (Psalm 104:1). Or he invites others to join him in worship: "Praise the LORD, all you nations! / Extol him, all you peoples!" (117:1); "Make a joyful noise to the LORD, all the earth" (100:1). Some of these hymns address God directly, while others speak of him in the third person.

Then these hymns declare various reasons for praising God, which are frequently introduced in the Hebrew by the emphatic word *ki*, meaning "because" or "for." Many of these declarations point to God's saving actions and awe-inspiring deeds on behalf of his chosen people or describe his acts as Creator and Lord of nature. Some statements of praise may reflect God's kingship and sovereignty over Israel or over the whole world; others proclaim and praise God's attributes of steadfast love, mercy, justice, wisdom, faithfulness, and so forth.

Psalm 98 "is a call to all people by those who have experienced God's saving presence and power in their lives, . . . an explosion in song and praise resulting from God's self-revelation, goodness and tenderness to his people," notes Msgr. John Sheridan in *Living the Psalms.* Opening with an invitation to sing the praises of the Lord, the psalm celebrates the "marvelous things" that God has done for Israel. The psalmist proclaims that the Lord, whom he portrays as a warrior, has acted in keeping with his covenant—that is, "he has remembered his steadfast love and faithfulness / to the house of Israel"—and declares that the whole earth recognizes God's victory (Psalm 98:1, 3).

> As we raise our voices to declare God's praises, we can also raise our hearts to him—hearts filled with love and adoration.

In verses 4–6, the psalmist urges all the earth to "make a joyful noise to the LORD," vocally with "joyous song" and "the sound of melody" as well as with musical instruments of all sorts. This exhortation to harmoniously orchestrated praise calls to mind the manner in which Israel worshipped in the Temple and at great festivals, acknowledging God as King and Lord.

Finally, the psalmist calls upon all of creation to acknowledge the Lord's presence and glorify him, for he is coming to judge the earth and establish his kingdom of justice and equity (Psalm 98:7-9). The images that personify nature—the sea roaring, floods clapping their hands, and hills singing together for joy—are some of the most poetic, beautiful, and exhilarating verses in the Book of Psalms.

Traditionally, Psalm 98 has been seen by the Church as a celebration of the coming of Christ in his incarnation and of his presence among us in the created world. Consequently, it has been given a place in the Christmas liturgy and throughout the octave of Christmas. The psalm also points to God's final coming. Scripture scholar Jean-Pierre Prévost has fittingly summed up its significance and unique power:

> We can truly speak of Psalm 98 as being an "unfinished symphony" meant to encourage among the faithful the joyful awaiting of God's coming at the end of time "to judge the world with righteousness, and the peoples with equity." Shall we join the chorus and the orchestra in such an uplifting symphony in honor of our God? (*God's Word Today*)

Understand!

1. What do you think the psalmist means by a "new" song (Psalm 98:1; see also Psalms 33:3; 96:1; 144:9)? What does the invitation to "sing a new song" suggest to you?

_____

_____

_____

_____

_____

2. What images are evoked by the expression "his [the Lord's] right hand and his holy arm" (Psalm 98:1; see also Exodus 15:6; Psalm 118:15-16; Isaiah 52:10)? In your opinion, what kind of "victory" is this psalm celebrating? Which verses in Psalm 98 support your opinion?

_____

_____

_____

_____

_____

_____

3. List the phrases the psalmist uses at the beginning (verses 1-3) and at the end (verse 9) of Psalm 98 to describe God's actions and his attributes. Which description speaks most personally to you? Why?

_____

_____

_____

_____

_____

_____

4. In addition to the psalmists, countless musicians, poets, and artists have also represented creation as participating in the praises of God. What songs, poems, and/or paintings can you think of that portray nature worshipping the Lord? In what ways does the world of nature influence and "shape" your prayer?

_____

_____

_____

_____

_____

5. Read Psalm 96 and Psalm 148, two other examples of hymns of praise. What features of these psalms are similar to those in Psalm 98? What additional insights into praising God do these psalms give you?

_____

_____

_____

_____

_____

_____

▶ In the Spotlight
Sing to the Lord!

[The psalms] were composed as poetry in song, and they attain their true meaning when they are sung in a contemplative fashion as pure praise of God. It is not necessary that they be sung in a beautiful and perfect manner, though this can enhance them as we try to pray. What really matters is that the psalms be sung humbly, prayerfully, slowly, and fervently. Only then can we begin to savor their richness, absorb their wisdom, and capture something of the pure joy of praising God.
—**Br. Victor-Antoine d'Avila-Latourrette**, *Blessings of the Daily*

What is a psalm but a musical instrument to give expression to all the virtues? The psalmist of old used it, with the aid of the Holy Spirit, to make earth reecho the music of heaven. He used the dead gut of strings to create harmony from a variety of notes, in order to send up to heaven the song of God's praise. In doing so, he taught us that we must first die to sin and then create in our lives on earth a harmony through virtuous deeds, if the grace of our devotion is to reach to the Lord.
—**St. Ambrose**, *Explanation of the Psalms*

Grow!

1. How has praising the Lord deepened your relationship with him? How often do you make worshipping God part of your daily prayer—beginning and ending the day with an act of praise? If it is not your practice to praise God in the morning and evening, ask the Holy Spirit to give you the desire to praise him and to develop this habit.

_____

_____

_____

_____

_____

_____

2. Recall a time when you were deeply moved to praise God without being self-conscious or inhibited. What led you to praise him so freely? Experiencing God's love and care for you? Being awed by God's greatness or the beauty of his creation? Realizing how he has saved you from a particular sin or personal failing?

_____

_____

_____

_____

_____

3. What physical actions do you use as expressions of praise when you pray? What impact do your gestures and posture in prayer have on you? How do you use music and song to enhance your worship?

_____

_____

_____

_____

_____

_____

4. Do you praise God only when you are emotionally "up" and happy
   about your life? How could the truth of your knowledge of God's
   unchanging love for you and his faithfulness help you worship him
   even when you feel downcast or "washed out"?

_____

_____

_____

_____

_____

5. In what ways do your relationship with God and your praise of
   him spill over into your daily life? Do you think others would recognize that you are a Christian by your attitudes and behavior?
   How does your life make the goodness of God present or apparent to others?

_____

_____

_____

_____

_____

▶In the Spotlight
Declaring God's Glory

Born in France in 1599, Blessed Marie of the Incarnation Guy-art entered an Ursuline convent after she was widowed. In 1639 she sailed to the New World, where she established the Ursu-lines in Quebec, Canada, and founded the oldest institution for women in North America. The order welcomed Algonquin and Iroquois students as well as Canadian-born French and Old World emigrants. During her long and adventuresome life—Marie died in 1672 at age seventy-three—the psalms fed her contemplative spirit and prayer, and were a source of strength, nourishment, and consolation to her.

In the psalms I saw God's justice, his judgments, his grandeur, his generosity. . . . I saw that the goodness of this divine spirit had established me in green and fertile pastures which kept my soul so nourished that it overflowed and I could not keep silent. . . .

This took me so completely out of myself that as I went about the monastery I was in a constant state of ecstasy. It was the same while I was at work. Sometimes my thoughts were concentrated on the purity of God and how all things declare his glory. The psalm "The heavens declare the glory of God" (Psalm 19) had an attraction for me which pierced my heart and enraptured my spirit. "Yes, yes, O my Love! 'Your testimonies are true; they are justified of themselves. They give witness to the foolish' (Psalm 19:8). Send me over the whole world to teach those who are ignorant of you!"

—Blessed Marie of the Incarnation, quoted in *The Saints' Guide to Learning to Pray*

Reflect!

1. The psalms reflect countless reasons to worship God and describe many of his praiseworthy attributes. Consider the particular personal reasons that you have to glorify and thank the Lord, or consider what attributes of God have touched you profoundly. You may find it helpful to note them in a journal or prayer diary so that you can easily call them to mind and let them shape your own prayers of praise.

2. Reflect on the following Scripture passages that portray how the Lord is glorified through song, music, and dance on the earth and in the heavens:

> When the horses of Pharaoh with his chariots and his chariot drivers went into the sea, the LORD brought back the waters of the sea upon them; but the Israelites walked through the sea on dry ground.
>
> Then the prophet Miriam, Aaron's sister, took a tambourine in her hand; and all the women went out after her with tambourines and with dancing. And Miriam sang to them:
>
> "Sing to the LORD, for he has triumphed gloriously;
> horse and rider he has thrown into the sea."
> (Exodus 15:19-21)

> David went and brought up the ark of God from the house of Obed-edom to the city of David with rejoicing; and when those who bore the ark of the LORD had gone six paces, he sacrificed an ox and a fatling. David danced before the LORD with all his might; David was girded with a linen ephod. So David and all the house of Israel brought up the ark of the LORD with shouting, and with the sound of the trumpet. (2 Samuel 6:12-15)

With gratitude in your hearts sing psalms, hymns, and spiritual songs to God. (Colossians 3:16)

And whenever the living creatures give glory and honor and thanks to the one who is seated on the throne, who lives forever and ever, the twenty-four elders fall before the one who is seated on the throne and worship the one who lives forever and ever; they cast their crowns before the throne, singing,

"You are worthy, our Lord and God,
to receive glory and honor and power,
for you created all things,
and by your will they existed and were created."
(Revelation 4:9-11)

▶ In the Spotlight
Telling the Praises of God

Francis of Assisi, one of the most universally beloved of the saints, took great delight in praising God. Like a troubadour, he went around the countryside joyously singing songs he composed to glorify the Lord. "The Praises of God," written by St. Francis to proclaim the Lord's greatness and grandeur, echo the praises found in so many of the ancient psalms.

Lord God:
you alone are holy,
you who work wonders!
You are strong, you are great,
you are the Most High,
you are the almighty King,
you, holy Father, King of heaven and earth.

Lord God: you are Three and you are One,
you are goodness, all goodness,
you are the highest Good,
Lord God, living and true.

You are love and charity, you are wisdom,
you are humility, you are patience,
you are beauty, you are sweetness,
you are safety, you are rest, you are joy,
you are our hope
and our delight,
you are justice, you are moderation
you are all our wealth
and riches overflowing.

You are beauty, you are gentleness,
you are our shelter, our guard
and our defender,
you are strength, you are refreshment,
you are our hope,
you are our faith,
you are our love,
you are our complete consolation,
you are our life everlasting,
great and wonderful Lord,
all powerful God, merciful Savior!
Amen.

—St. Francis of Assisi

Act!

Take a walk and contemplate the beauty of God's creation. Like St. Francis of Assisi, spontaneously pray—perhaps even sing or shout aloud—your own psalm of praise, magnifying the Lord for all the wonders of nature that you see around you.

▶ In the Spotlight
Biblical Canticles of Praise

Besides those in the Book of Psalms, many other songs of praise can be found throughout the Old and New Testaments. These sacred poems and hymns, commonly called "canticles" (from Latin, *canticulum*, "little song"), celebrate God's steadfast love, his goodness, and his mighty deeds to save and deliver his people. Many of these canticles are heard in the Liturgy of the Word at Mass or prayed in the Liturgy of the Hours.

Some notable examples of biblical canticles are Moses' song of deliverance (Exodus 15:1-18), Judith's victory hymn (Judith 16:2-3, 13-15), the thanksgiving song of the redeemed (Isaiah 12:1-6), Mary's Magnificat (Luke 1:47-55), and various songs in the Book of Revelation (for example, 12:10-12; 15:3-4; and 19:1-7). The following selection of verses is from the Old Testament canticle that was sung by the three young men whom God preserved when they were thrown into the fiery furnace because they refused to worship the golden statue set up by King Nebuchadnezzar.

Blessed are you, O Lord, God of our ancestors,
  and to be praised and highly exalted forever;

And blessed is your glorious, holy name,
 and to be highly praised and highly exalted forever.

Let the earth bless the Lord;
 let it sing praise to him and highly exalt him forever.

Bless the Lord, all people on earth;
 sing praise to him and highly exalt him forever.

Bless the Lord, Hananiah, Azariah, and Mishael;
 sing praise to him and highly exalt him forever.
For he has rescued us from Hades and saved us from the
  power of death,
 and delivered us from the midst of the burning fiery
  furnace;
 from the midst of the fire he has delivered us.
Give thanks to the Lord, for he is good,
 for his mercy endures forever.
—Daniel 3:52, 74, 82, 88-89

"Out of the Depths I Cry to You, O Lord"

Psalm 130:1-8

¹ Out of the depths I cry to you, O LORD.
  ² Lord, hear my voice!
Let your ears be attentive
    to the voice of my supplications!

³ If you, O LORD, should mark iniquities,
    Lord, who could stand?
⁴ But there is forgiveness with you,
    so that you may be revered.

> If you want to flee from God, flee to Him instead. Flee to Him by confessing to Him; don't flee from Him by trying to hide. For you can't hide, but you can confess.
> —**St. Augustine**

⁵ I wait for the LORD, my soul waits,
    and in his word I hope;
⁶ my soul waits for the Lord
    more than those who watch for the morning,
    more than those who watch for the morning.

⁷ O Israel, hope in the LORD!
    For with the LORD there is steadfast love,
    and with him is great power to redeem.
⁸ It is he who will redeem Israel
    from all its iniquities.

Mankind's relationship with God was broken by Adam and Eve's sinful disobedience, but through the atoning death of Jesus and his resurrection, sin-ridden humanity was reconciled to God. Through the shedding of his blood, Jesus removed our condemnation and offered us forgiveness. Yet God calls us to repent of the personal sins and offenses that we commit and that separate us from him. "Guilt must not be allowed to fester in the silence of the soul, poisoning it from within," writes Pope Benedict XVI in *Jesus of*

Nazareth—Holy Week: From the Entrance into Jerusalem to the Resurrection. "It needs to be confessed. Through confession we bring it to the light, we place it in Christ's purifying love (cf. John 3:20-21)."

The fullest meaning of repentance involves a dual choice: to turn *away* from sin and to turn *toward* God. When we repent, moved by sorrow and remorse, we show, not only a change of heart, mind, and behavior, but a fidelity to God and the desire and intention to set aside sin and live by his commandments and standards. God's forgiveness is inseparably linked with our repentance: "If we confess our sins, he who is faithful and just will forgive us our sins and cleanse us from all unrighteousness" (1 John 1:9). This forgiveness brings to fullness in us the work of transformation and healing begun by our repentance.

The Book of Psalms gives us profound words in which to acknowledge our sin before God as well as a way to express the confidence and joy of knowing his steadfast love and forgiveness. Seven psalms are particularly expressive of sorrow for sin (6, 32, 38, 51, 102, 130, and 143) and have been designated by Church tradition since the sixth century as "penitential psalms" or "psalms of confession." Among them is Psalm 130, called in Latin the *De Profundis* for its opening words, "Out of the depths." A heartfelt request for pardon and mercy, it is prayed in the funeral liturgy of the Church and in the Office for the Dead and is frequently repeated in the Liturgy of the Hours. Yet, as Br. Victor-Antoine d'Avila-Latourette has so insightfully noted, Psalm 130

> is above all a prayer that opens new horizons, for it is a prayer that expresses conversion. Conversion is a long and arduous road, a road that demands all the inner energies of our being as we seek to traverse it. *Out of the depths I cry to you, O Lord.* The more our cry leaps out from the depths of our misery, the more honest the cry and the more genuine our heart's attitude. It is then when we find who and what we truly are. (*Blessings of the Daily*)

Although its author is unknown, scholars surmise that Psalm 130 was probably composed during the Babylonian Exile, or perhaps for the day of penance prescribed by the priest Ezra when the Jewish exiles returned to Jerusalem (Ezra 9:5-15). The sufferings and misery that the people had experienced during the exile had brought them to the confession of their guilt and had stirred in their hearts both fresh hope of a redeemer and confidence in God's mercy.

Through Jesus' redeeming sacrifice, we have been reborn to hope and can now confess our sins to our Father with confidence that he forgives us.

The psalmist cries to God from the "depths" of his need and distress, experiencing great spiritual misery for his sins—whatever they may have been. Moved to genuine sorrow, he humbly asks to be heard (Psalm 130:1-2). Yet he is also at the height of confidence as he seeks forgiveness for his transgressions because he trusts in the loving kindness and mercy of the Lord. Certain that he will not be doomed or condemned, he joyfully asserts, "If you, O LORD, should mark iniquities, / Lord, who could stand? / But there is forgiveness with you, / so that you may be revered" (verses 3-4). God is unfailing in his love and compassion toward those who have fallen and confess their sin.

Then the psalmist paints a beautiful picture of vibrant hope: "My soul waits for the Lord / more than those who watch for the morning" (Psalm 130:6). The light and warmth of God's love and forgiveness will shine on him like the rising sun at dawn! Finally, in the closing verses of this psalm, which is both a sincere and honest confession of sin and a profound profession of faith, we find once again the Hebrew word *hesed*—"with the LORD there is steadfast love" (verse 7). The psalmist realizes that God's *hesed* is the reason that he and his fellow Israelites have been forgiven and redeemed (verse 8). (Note that he prays not only on his own behalf but with and on behalf of his community.)

Who of us is not occasionally in the depths, sorely in need of repentance? But through Jesus' redeeming sacrifice, we have been reborn to hope and can now confess our sins to our Father with confidence that he forgives us.

Understand!

1. What personal character traits and emotions of the psalmist are evident in Psalm 130? What aspects of the psalm indicate that the psalmist is praying not only for himself but for the whole community? How does this show his solidarity with God's people?

   _____

   _____

   _____

   _____

   _____

2. Why do you think the psalmist repeats his request that God hear his voice in verses 1 and 2 and again uses repetition in verse 6? How do these repetitions affect you when you pray this psalm? Do you often "repeat yourself" in your prayers and petitions to God? Why or why not?

   _____

   _____

   _____

   _____

   _____

3. What thoughts do the visual images of "crying from the depths" (verse 1) and "watching for the morning" (verse 6) evoke in you? In what ways do these images effectively reflect the condition that the psalmist is in? Read Psalm 119:123, Isaiah 52:7-8, and Isaiah 62:6-7 to enhance your understanding of watching and being a watchman.

_____

_____

_____

_____

4. What benefits is the psalmist waiting for and hoping to receive from God (Psalm 130:5-8)? Why, in your opinion, is the psalmist so confident of God's *hesed*—mercy and steadfast love—and redemption?

_____

_____

_____

_____

5. Many other psalms also speak of "waiting for the Lord" (for example, Psalms 27:14; 33:20; 40:1; 62:1). What disposition and attitudes are required by one who "waits" on the Lord? What further insights do the following texts give you regarding waiting: Isaiah 40:31; Habakkuk 2:3; Romans 8:19; James 5:7?

_____

_____

_____

_____

_____

_____

▶ In the Spotlight
"My Life's on the Line before God"

Over the centuries, Scripture scholars, linguists, and poets have translated the ancient Hebrew words of the psalms into many languages, trying to retain their original meaning and beauty while also making them understandable and relevant to the mentality of the current era. Sometimes we become so used to a familiar translation that we pray the Scripture passage by rote, perhaps without thinking about its meaning. Using a different translation with a slightly different way of phrasing that passage can give us fresh insights into its meaning. A more contemporary translation may also provide a new understanding of outmoded words whose meanings elude us today. This rendering of Psalm 130 is from The Message, *a modern paraphrase of Scripture that is called by its publisher, NavPress, "the Bible in contemporary language":*

Help GOD—the bottom has fallen out of my life!
    Master, hear my cry for help!
Listen hard! Open your ears!
    Listen to my cries for mercy.

If you, GOD, kept records on wrongdoings,
    who would stand a chance?
As it turns out, forgiveness is your habit,
    and that's why you're worshiped.

I pray to GOD—my life a prayer—
    and wait for what he'll say and do.
My life's on the line before God, my Lord,
    waiting and watching till morning,
    waiting and watching till morning.

Oh Israel, wait and watch for God—
  with GOD's arrival comes love,
  with GOD's arrival comes generous redemption.
No doubt about it—he'll redeem Israel,
  buy back Israel from captivity to sin.
—**Translation by Eugene H. Peterson**

Grow!

1. How does the awareness of your sins affect you? Do despair or feelings of guilt and unworthiness keep you from turning to God? How can sorrow and a humble recognition of your sinfulness lead you to confess your sin and ask God for forgiveness and the grace to change?

_____

_____

_____

_____

_____

2. From what "depths" (Psalm 130:1) in your life have you cried out to God? How did God "hear your voice" and your "supplications" (130:2)? In what ways did God answer you?

_____

_____

_____

_____

_____

3. Do you feel that the Lord "marks your iniquities" (Psalm 130:3), that is, holds your sins against you like "black marks" in his ledger or record book? Is it difficult for you to believe that God is merciful and forgiving? If so, why? What assures you that God continues to love you even when you have sinned against him?

---

4. Recall a time when an area of your life was transformed by your repentance and the experience of God's forgiveness. What fruit did this bear? What are your feelings when you receive absolution for your sins in the Sacrament of Reconciliation? Joy at knowing you are forgiven? A sense of being cleansed? Relief? Gratitude? Reverence for the Lord (Psalm 130:4)?

---

5. Have you ever asked forgiveness of another person for a grave offense you committed against him or her? Have you ever extended forgiveness to someone who has seriously wronged or injured you? Did this give you a deeper understanding of God's heart and compassion? In what other ways did this experience affect you?

▶In the Spotlight
Pardon Me, Lord!

Asking for pardon is the first step in building a relationship with God. The only way that you will ever enter into an intimate relationship with God, a relationship where you experience God's abundance and blessing, is to first confess your sins. That's why it's so important. It's what makes it possible for you to pray all the other prayers and, most specifically, to ask that God's will be done in your life. Once you've asked for forgiveness, then you can begin to ask God to show you what direction he wants you to move in. Asking for forgiveness enables God to change your life. By simply and humbly confessing your failings, you put yourself in the place where God's YES resounds throughout creation.

Isn't this what you really want? To be in a place where everything works according to God's perfect plan?

Of course you do. That's what we all want, deep down: to be so in sync with God that what we want is the same thing that God wants. So begin now by asking pardon for having placed yourself outside of God's eternal perfect goodness. You don't have to don sackcloth and ashes or wail aloud on the side of the road as they did in ancient times. All you must do is sincerely and honestly admit that at times you have done the things you know you shouldn't have done and at other times you haven't done the things you know you should have. If you are in a state of serious discord with God, in what is called mortal sin, the Sacrament of Confession is literally a godsend. Even if you aren't in that state, going to confession can help give you the reassurance you may need that God has indeed granted you pardon.

—**Woodeene Koenig-Bricker,** *Asking God for the Gifts He Wants to Give You*

Reflect!

1. Psalm 32 teaches us some valuable lessons by contrasting the refusal to acknowledge our sins with the happiness of confessing them and receiving God's forgiveness:

> Happy are those whose transgression is forgiven,
>   whose sin is covered.
> Happy are those to whom the LORD imputes no iniquity,
>   and in whose spirit there is no deceit.
>
> While I kept silence, my body wasted away
>   through my groaning all day long.
> For day and night your hand was heavy upon me;
>   my strength was dried up as by the heat of summer.
>
> Then I acknowledged my sin to you,
>   and I did not hide my iniquity;
> I said, "I will confess my transgressions to the LORD,"
>   and you forgave the guilt of my sin. (Psalm 32:1-5)

Are there sins that you are refusing to acknowledge and turn away from? Ask the Holy Spirit to give you the clarity and strength—and deep love for God—to enable you to repent and confess your sins.

2. Reflect on the following Scripture passages that portray God's call to us to confess our sinfulness and remind us of his mercy and forgiveness:

> Yet even now, says the LORD,
>   return to me with all your heart,
> with fasting, with weeping, and with mourning;
>   rend your hearts and not your clothing.

Return to the LORD, your God,
    for he is gracious and merciful,
slow to anger, and abounding in steadfast love,
    and relents from punishing. (Joel 2:12-13)

As Jesus was walking along, he saw a man called Matthew sitting at the tax booth; and he said to him, "Follow me." And he got up and followed him.

And as he sat at dinner in the house, many tax collectors and sinners came and were sitting with him and his disciples. When the Pharisees saw this, they said to his disciples, "Why does your teacher eat with tax collectors and sinners?" But when he heard this, he said, "Those who are well have no need of a physician, but those who are sick. Go and learn what this means, 'I desire mercy, not sacrifice.' For I have come to call not the righteous but sinners." (Matthew 9:9-13)

John [the Baptist] said to the crowds that came out to be baptized by him, ". . . Bear fruits worthy of repentance." (Luke 3:7, 8)

Now all the tax collectors and sinners were coming near to listen to him. And the Pharisees and the scribes were grumbling and saying, "This fellow welcomes sinners and eats with them."

So he told them this parable: "Which one of you, having a hundred sheep and losing one of them, does not leave the ninety-nine in the wilderness and go after the one that is lost until he finds it? When he has found it, he lays it on his shoulders and rejoices. And when he comes home, he calls together his friends and neighbors, saying to them, 'Rejoice with me, for I have found my sheep that was lost.' Just so, I tell you, there will be more joy in heaven over one sinner who repents than over ninety-nine righteous people who need no repentance." (Luke 15:1-7)

▶ In the Spotlight
The Liturgy of the Hours

Many psalms had a prominent place in the liturgical prayers used in the services in the ancient Temple in Jerusalem. Later, when the early Christians began meeting together for worship, they naturally imitated the worship of their Jewish brothers and sisters—for example, the apostles observed the Jewish custom of praying at the third, sixth, and ninth hour, and at midnight (Acts 10:3, 9; 16:25). As Christianity began to separate from Judaism, the practice of praying at fixed times continued. And as the prayer services of the Christians evolved, readings from the Gospels, Acts, and epistles were added to the recital or chanting of psalms and the reading of the Hebrew Scriptures. Out of these practices developed the Liturgy of the Hours (Latin: *liturgia horarum*), also known as the Divine Office (Latin: *Officium Divinum*).

The Desert Fathers and St. Benedict—considered the "Father of Western Monasticism"—contributed to the basic organization of the Liturgy of the Hours, which by the end of the eighth century was composed of eight offices: Matins (during the night), Lauds (dawn), Prime (early morning), Terce (midmorning), Sext (midday), None (midafternoon), Vespers (evening), and Compline (night). After the Second Vatican Council, Pope Paul VI introduced a restructuring of the Divine Office, with a revision of the prayers and a new distribution of the psalms—in brief, the hours were defined as "major" and "minor," with Prime entirely eliminated. The major hours consist of the Office of Readings as well as Morning Prayer (Lauds) and Evening Prayer (Vespers). The Office of Readings can be used at any time of the day. The character of Morning Prayer is that of praise, while that of Evening Prayer is of thanksgiving. In this "new" Liturgy of the Hours, the period over which the entire Psalter is recited was extended from one week to four.

Together with the Mass, the Liturgy of the Hours constitutes the official public prayer life of the Catholic Church. This set of daily prayers is recited daily by the clergy as well as members of religious and monastic institutes. Drawn to this regular form of prayer, countless lay Catholics have also taken up this practice.

Act!

St. John Vianney (1786–1859), universal patron saint of priests, was renowned for his extraordinary ministry in the confessional. Thousands flocked from every region of France to his parish in Ars to receive the Sacrament of Reconciliation. He was said to occasionally read the consciences, see the past sins, and predict the future of his penitents. On many days he spent up to seventeen hours hearing confessions. Urging people to come to confession, St. John Vianney said, "My children, when we have a little stain on our souls, we must do like someone who has a beautiful crystal globe of which she takes great care. If the globe gets a little dusty, when she sees it, she will pass a sponge over it, and here is the globe bright and shining again."

Make a sincere examination of conscience, asking the Holy Spirit to show you any areas of your life where you are in need of repentance and God's forgiveness. Then reflect on one of the penitential psalms (6, 32, 38, 51, 102, 130, or 143). If possible, receive the Sacrament of Reconciliation this week.

▶ In the Spotlight
"Have Mercy on Me, O God"

Psalm 51, often called the Miserere *(Latin: "have mercy") after its opening words, "Have mercy on me, O God," is perhaps the best known of the penitential psalms because it has a prominent place in the liturgical services during Lent and Holy Week and in the Liturgy of the Hours. In some Jewish rituals, this psalm is recited on the Day of Atonement.*

Tradition holds Psalm 51 to be David's prayer of repentance after he was reproached by the prophet Nathan for committing adultery with Bathsheba and having her husband, Uriah, killed (2 Samuel 11–12). Here, popular Scripture commentator George Martin offers his personal comments on this psalm:

Psalm 51 is my favorite psalm for coming before God in admission of sin, for it plainly admits my sin before God and acknowledges that he would be entirely justified in passing sentence on me.

Yet Psalm 51 is a psalm of hope and confidence in God as well as a psalm acknowledging guilt. It asks mercy from a God of goodness and tenderness, a God who is willing to forgive and purify. It approaches God with confidence, expecting him to give joy and gladness through his forgiveness.

The forgiveness that Psalm 51 asks is not merely the wiping out of sin but also the positive gift of the Holy Spirit, creating a new heart in us and bringing us into God's presence. We are reminded of the Exultet, the prayer of the Easter Vigil that calls Adam's sin a "happy fault" because it was the occasion of so great a redemption as we received in Jesus Christ. To come to God in repentance is not only to turn away from our sins but to turn toward him, accepting the gift of his mercy, accepting his gift of eternal life.
—**George Martin,** *God's Word Today*

"I Give You Thanks, O Lord"

Psalm 138:1-8

¹ I give you thanks, O LORD, with my whole heart;
  before the gods I sing your praise;
² I bow down toward your holy temple
  and give thanks to your name for your steadfast love and
    your faithfulness;
  for you have exalted your name
    and your word
  above everything.
³ On the day I called, you
    answered me,
  you increased my strength of
    soul.

> Thanksgiving is generated by the contemplation of God's goodness and greatness and faithfulness.
> —**St. John Cassian**

⁴ All the kings of the earth shall praise you, O LORD,
  for they have heard the words of your mouth.
⁵ They shall sing of the ways of the LORD,
  for great is the glory of the LORD.
⁶ For though the LORD is high, he regards the lowly;
  but the haughty he perceives from far away.

⁷ Though I walk in the midst of trouble,
  you preserve me against the wrath of my enemies;
 you stretch out your hand,
  and your right hand delivers me.
⁸ The LORD will fulfill his purpose for me;
  your steadfast love, O LORD, endures forever.
  Do not forsake the work of your hands.

J ust as God delights in our worship, so, too, does he delight in our thanks. Expressions of gratitude are found in many psalms that are hymns of praise—and giving thanks to God is essentially the same as praising and lauding him, for in all these vocal acts we are acknowledging the greatness of the Lord and his fidelity, goodness, favor, and benefits to us. Yet psalms of thanksgiving are recognized as a distinct literary genre because they chiefly express gratitude for a specific circumstance, such as help received at a time of need, deliverance from trials or enemies, healing of illness, or relief from anguish.

In ancient Israel, individuals wishing to show gratitude to God would normally visit the Temple in Jerusalem, where they accompanied their prayer by a "thank offering." This was followed by a meal in which they feasted on the sacrificial offering—a lamb or bull. Those present in the Temple area, especially the poor, were invited to take part in the feast. In this way, the person giving thanks publicly testified to God's goodness. Among psalms of individual thanksgiving are Psalms 9, 30, 92, 100, 103, 116, and 138. Some of the psalms are communal or national hymns of thanksgiving (for example, Psalms 65, 66, 75, 118, 124, and 136), where God's saving deeds on behalf of his entire people are recalled. Often these communal psalms include narratives that give a historical survey (as in 107) and may have been composed for use at liturgical celebrations or days of national public thanksgiving.

Although authorship of Psalm 138 is attributed by Jewish tradition to David or his patronage, most likely it was composed in a later epoch. The psalm opens with a wholehearted expression of gratitude as the psalmist praises the Lord for his steadfast love and faithfulness. He sings before God, who is in heaven with his court of angels (verses 1-2). (The "gods" of verse 1 were understood by the ancient Israelites to be the deities worshipped by the surrounding nations and were considered less powerful than Israel's God. After the Babylonian Exile, as Israel's monotheistic belief in God as the sole deity grew, these "gods" were understood to be angels.) The psalmist also bows toward the earthly Temple in Jerusalem, knowing that the Lord listens to prayer there too.

Next, the psalmist recalls that God had heard his cry and helped him in past afflictions, giving him strength (verse 3). Then he looks beyond his own personal needs, broadening his vision outward, to declare that others—"the kings of the earth"—will also recognize the ways of the Lord, acknowledge his greatness, and glorify him (verses 4-5). It's also recognized that although the Lord is "high"—mighty and sovereign over all that he has created—he cares for the "lowly" who are in distress (verse 6). The psalmist then again gives personal testimony, declaring that when he is in trouble, the Lord stretches out his hand to deliver him (verse 7).

> Just as God delights in our worship, so, too, does he delight in our thanks.

Finally, convinced that the Lord will fulfill his purpose for him and will never forsake him (verse 8), the psalmist places complete confidence in God. Just as the psalm began with a heartfelt acknowledgment of God's steadfast love and faithfulness (verse 2), it ends in a exultant crescendo proclaiming that this love—*hesed*, in Hebrew—will endure forever.

As Pope Benedict XVI noted in a homily on Psalm 138, "The finale of the Psalm, then, is a last passionate profession of trust in God whose goodness is eternal: he will not 'discard . . . the work of [his] hands,' in other words, his creature (verse 8). And we, too, must live in this trust, in this certainty of God's goodness." The pope concluded,

> We must be sure that however burdensome and tempestuous the trials that await us may be, we will never be left on our own, we will never fall out of the Lord's hands, those hands that created us and now sustain us on our journey through life. As St.

Paul was to confess: "he who has begun the good work in you will carry it through to completion" (Philippians 1:6). (General Audience, December 7, 2005)

Understand!

1. List the phrases in Psalm 138 that describe the psalmist's posture and feelings toward God. How is his prayer active? What "body language" does he use?

_____

_____

_____

_____

_____

2. What verbs does the psalmist use in Psalm 138 to describe God's actions? What adjectives does he use to illustrate God's character? What do these descriptive words reveal about God's disposition toward those who call upon him?

_____

_____

_____

_____

_____

3. For what particular gifts or deeds of God does the psalmist express his gratitude?

_____

_____

_____

_____

_____

_____

4. How does Psalm 138 depict an interplay between faith and gratitude? In the psalmist's prayer, what relationship between past, present, and future actions of God is made apparent?

_____

_____

_____

_____

_____

_____

5. Read and reflect on another psalm of thanksgiving (for example, Psalm 9, 30, 92, 100, 103, or 116). What elements does this psalm have in common with Psalm 138? What expressions of gratitude in it expand on those you have already seen in Psalm 138?

_____

_____

_____

_____

_____

_____

▶ In the Spotlight
Enter His Gates with Thanksgiving!

Psalms of praise and thanksgiving can lift our spirits, as the Christian writer Hannah Whitall Smith urges us to do with Psalm 100:

Make a joyful noise to the LORD, all the earth.
  Worship the LORD with gladness;
  come into his presence with singing.

Know that the LORD is God.
  It is he that made us, and we are his;
  we are his people, and the sheep of his pasture.

Enter his gates with thanksgiving,
  and his courts with praise.
  Give thanks to him, bless his name.

For the LORD is good;
  his steadfast love endures forever,
  and his faithfulness to all generations. (Psalm 100:1-5)

We are commanded to enter into God's gates with thanksgiving and into his courts with praise, and I am convinced that the giving of thanks is the key that opens these gates more quickly than anything else. Try it. The next time you feel dead, cold, and low-spirited, begin to praise and thank the Lord. Enumerate to yourself the benefits he has bestowed upon you, and thank him heartily for each one, and see if your spirits do not begin to rise and your heart get warmed up.

Sometimes you may feel too disheartened to pray; then try giving thanks instead. Before you know it, you will find yourself glad and thankful for all God's loving-kindness and his tender mercies.

—**Hannah Whitall Smith**, *Daily He Leads Me*

Grow!

1. How large a part does thanksgiving play in your relationship with the Lord? How does a sense of gratitude to God affect your daily life? What happens when you lose your sense of gratitude?

_____

_____

_____

_____

_____

2. How confident are you of God's concern and loving care for you? What effect does this knowledge have on you? How open and eager are you to tell others about God's blessing and how he is at work in your life?

_____

_____

_____

_____

_____

3. In addition to vocal prayers, what else might you offer to the Lord in gratitude? Your talents to serve him and to reach out to others? Your time and energy? Your financial resources?

_____

_____

_____

_____

_____

4. Song, music, dance, and festive meals can all be expressions of gratitude. How can you make more use of such meaningful actions to give thanks to God? What events might you celebrate with your family or friends as a way of thanking God?

_____

_____

_____

_____

_____

_____

5. Do trials or calamities in your life undermine your faith in God and gratitude to him? How can you maintain a faith-filled and thankful attitude when you encounter challenges or troubles? Recall an occasion when you gave thanks in the midst of a misfortune. How did this transform your outlook or change the situation?

_____

_____

_____

_____

_____

_____

▶ In the Spotlight
Hebrew Words of Thanks

Yadah, the Hebrew verb meaning "to give thanks, laud, praise," is a key word in the language of worship. _Yadah_ is used nearly 120 times in the Hebrew Scriptures, including more than seventy times in the Book of Psalms, to express gratitude to God in ritual or public worship as well as personal praise of God (for example, 30:12 and 35:18). Thanksgiving is frequently directed in particular to the name of the Lord (106:47; 122:4).

The Hebrew noun *todah* appears more than thirty times in the Old Testament to indicate "thanksgiving" in hymns, psalms, and canticles of worship (for example, Psalms 26:7; 42:4). In addition, the word is used to refer to the thanksgiving choir or procession (Nehemiah 12:31, 38) and the thanksgiving offering designated in Leviticus 7:12. *Todah* has been preserved in modern Hebrew as the customary word for saying "Thank you."

Reflect!

1. Search your heart and ask the Holy Spirit to reveal to you any disposition or attitudes that keep you from recognizing God's blessings and provisions and that block you from experiencing and expressing gratitude. This might be, for example, pride, lethargy, discontent, complaining, taking God's gifts for granted, or holding on to your own agenda. What could you do to overcome such obstacles?

2. Reflect on the following Scripture passages that portray expressions of gratitude to God:

> Then David blessed the LORD in the presence of all the assembly; David said: "Blessed are you, O LORD, the God of our ancestor Israel, forever and ever. Yours, O LORD, are the greatness, the power, the glory, the victory, and the majesty; for all that is in the heavens and on the earth is yours; yours is the kingdom, O LORD, and you are exalted as head above all. Riches and honor come from you, and you rule over all. In your hand are power and might; and it is in your hand to make great and to give strength to all. And now, our God, we give thanks to you and praise your glorious name." (1 Chronicles 29:10-13)

I will give thanks to the LORD with my whole heart;
    I will tell of all your wonderful deeds.
I will be glad and exult in you;
    I will sing praise to your name, O Most High.
(Psalm 9:1-2)

Give thanks to the LORD,
    call on his name;
make known his deeds among the nations;
    proclaim that his name is exalted. (Isaiah 12:4)

Be filled with the Spirit, as you sing psalms and hymns and spiritual songs among yourselves, singing and making melody to the Lord in your hearts, giving thanks to God the Father at all times and for everything in the name of our Lord Jesus Christ. (Ephesians 5:18-20)

Rejoice always, pray without ceasing, give thanks in all circumstances; for this is the will of God in Christ Jesus for you. (1 Thessalonians 5:16-18)

▶ In the Spotlight
The Great Hallel

O give thanks to the LORD, for he is good,
    for his steadfast love endures forever.
O give thanks to the God of gods,
    for his steadfast love endures forever.
O give thanks to the Lord of lords,
    for his steadfast love endures forever;

who alone does great wonders,
    for his steadfast love endures forever;

who by understanding made the heavens,
for his steadfast love endures forever; . . .

who divided the Red Sea in two,
for his steadfast love endures forever;
and made Israel pass through the midst of it,
for his steadfast love endures forever;
but overthrew Pharaoh and his army in the Red Sea,
for his steadfast love endures forever;
who led his people through the wilderness,
for his steadfast love endures forever; . . .

It is he who remembered us in our low estate,
for his steadfast love endures forever;
and rescued us from our foes,
for his steadfast love endures forever;
who gives food to all flesh,
for his steadfast love endures forever.

O give thanks to the God of heaven,
for his steadfast love endures forever.
(Psalm 136:1-5, 13-16, 23-26)

Psalm 136 is known in the Jewish Psalter as the "Great Hallel"—
the "Great Psalm of Praise"—and is recited by devout Jews every
Sabbath and at Passover. It contemplates the wonders of God's
creation and recounts God's deliverance of Israel from bondage
in Egypt, the miraculous crossing of the Red Sea, and the entry
into the Promised Land. These events prefigure our redemption in Christ, so Christians also cherish this psalm. The final
verses of the psalm remind us that the God who saved Israel is
the same God who saves us.

The psalm was originally designed to be prayed as a litany
as the Israelites gathered in the Temple. The priest or worship
leader proclaimed the first line of each verse and the congregation

responded with the recurring refrain: "For his steadfast love endures forever." The Hebrew word for this steadfast love is *hesed*—God's covenant loyalty, the kind of loving kindness and mercy that is constant, enduring, unfailing, and faithful.

The sheer force of the repetition of this refrain—no less than twenty-six times!—drives the truth of God's *hesed* home to us. Each of the psalm's successive verses gives us further reason to praise God for his saving deeds.

Act!

Bless the LORD, O my soul,
  and all that is within me,
  bless his holy name.
Bless the LORD, O my soul,
  and do not forget all his benefits—
who forgives all your iniquity,
  who heals all your diseases,
who redeems your life from the Pit,
  who crowns you with steadfast love and mercy,
who satisfies you with good as long as you live
  so that your youth is renewed like the eagle's. (Psalm 103:1-5)

Reflect on your personal "salvation history"—those particular ways that God has acted on your behalf. As you recall the various blessings and gifts that you have received from the Lord, thank him for each of them and express your gratitude to him. You may find it helpful to use Psalm 136, the Great Hallel, or Psalm 103 as a model for your prayer. You may even want to write your own psalm of thanksgiving.

▶ In the Spotlight
Thanksgiving, Praise, and the Eucharist

There is no better way to praise God than to celebrate and receive the Eucharist. The Catechism of the Catholic Church *explains how the Eucharist is a sacrifice of praise and thanksgiving to the Father:*

The Eucharist, the sacrament of our salvation accomplished by Christ on the cross, is also a sacrifice of praise in thanksgiving for the work of creation. In the Eucharistic sacrifice the whole of creation loved by God is presented to the Father through the death and the Resurrection of Christ. Through Christ the Church can offer the sacrifice of praise in thanksgiving for all that God has made good, beautiful, and just in creation and in humanity.

The Eucharist is a sacrifice of thanksgiving to the Father, a blessing by which the Church expresses her gratitude to God for all his benefits, for all that he has accomplished through creation, redemption, and sanctification. Eucharist means first of all "thanksgiving."

The Eucharist is also the sacrifice of praise by which the Church sings the glory of God in the name of all creation. This sacrifice of praise is possible only through Christ: he unites the faithful to his person, to his praise, and to his intercession, so that the sacrifice of praise to the Father is offered *through* Christ and *with* him, to be accepted *in* him. (1359–61)

"My Soul Is Cast Down within Me"

Psalm 42:1-11

¹ As a deer longs for flowing streams,
    so my soul longs for you, O God.
² My soul thirsts for God,
    for the living God.
When shall I come and behold
    the face of God?
³ My tears have been my food
    day and night,
while people say to me continually,
    "Where is your God?"

⁴ These things I remember,
    as I pour out my soul:
how I went with the throng,
    and led them in procession to the house of God,
with glad shouts and songs of thanksgiving,
    a multitude keeping festival.
⁵ Why are you cast down, O my soul,
    and why are you disquieted within me?
Hope in God; for I shall again praise him,
    my help ⁶ and my God.

My soul is cast down within me;
    therefore I remember you
from the land of Jordan and of Hermon,
    from Mount Mizar.
⁷ Deep calls to deep
    at the thunder of your cataracts;
all your waves and your billows
    have gone over me.
⁸ By day the LORD commands his steadfast love,

This psalm, with its poetic, picturesque mood, is strangely relevant to how we feel when God seems absent, when the death of a friend, the collapse of our health, or the disintegration of a dream tempts us to a terrible sense of futility.
—Msgr. John Sheridan

and at night his song is with me,
    a prayer to the God of my life.

[9] I say to God, my rock,
    "Why have you forgotten me?
Why must I walk about mournfully
    because the enemy oppresses me?"
[10] As with a deadly wound in my body,
    my adversaries taunt me,
while they say to me continually,
    "Where is your God?"

[11] Why are you cast down, O my soul,
    and why are you disquieted within me?
Hope in God; for I shall again praise him,
    my help and my God.

Psalm 43:1-5

[1] Vindicate me, O God, and defend my cause
    against an ungodly people;
from those who are deceitful and unjust
    deliver me!
[2] For you are the God in whom I take refuge;
    why have you cast me off?
Why must I walk about mournfully
    because of the oppression of the enemy?

[3] O send out your light and your truth;
    let them lead me;
let them bring me to your holy hill
    and to your dwelling.
[4] Then I will go to the altar of God,

to God my exceeding joy;
and I will praise you with the harp,
    O God, my God.

5 Why are you cast down, O my soul,
    and why are you disquieted within me?
Hope in God; for I shall again praise him,
    my help and my God.

While there are numerous hymns of praise and thanksgiving in the Psalter, petitions and laments form the largest single category of psalms. These entreaties are moving prayers that reflect the challenge of honoring God when difficulties arise. They express the reality of life's struggles—day-to-day temptations as well as major setbacks and failings—in a world that has been infected by mankind's sin.

Many of the laments in the psalms concern the supplicant's own circumstances—for example, personal sufferings and troubles; life-threatening sickness; or persecution, harassment, or false accusations brought against him by his enemies. These individual prayers are composed in the first person as heartfelt cries for God to come to the psalmist's aid in misfortune. Typically, they open with an appeal or invocation to God; then follows a description of the distress and a request for the needed help—perhaps for healing, for rescue, or for vindication. At times the prayer includes an admission of sin (seen as the cause of the trouble) and a plea for forgiveness, while at other times there is an assertion of innocence and righteousness. Frequently, the psalmist states reasons why the Lord should hear his prayer, citing his own fidelity or recalling God's covenant promises. Such entreaties commonly end with gratitude or an exuberant proclamation of God's glory. Though the supplicant expresses pain and deep personal anguish, his prayer is never without some trace of hope and trust in

God and an expression of confidence that God has heard his cries and will deliver or save him.

Other laments—among them Psalms 44, 60, 74, 79, 85, and 137—are expressed in the collective "we," the public voice of the community or the nation. When facing some grave catastrophe such as war, invasion, epidemic, flood, or drought, God's people join in communal petitions that are often accompanied by fasting or other penitential practices (for example, wearing sackcloth and ashes) in acknowledgment of their sinfulness. And when asking for help, the supplicants stress the Lord's faithfulness and recall his historic acts of salvation.

> This ardent prayer of an exiled Israelite reflects the prayer of all who long to see God and yearn for their heavenly homeland.

Psalms 42 and 43 were originally a single poem, sharing a single meter and united theme. The highly lyrical style of this lament of one living near Israel's northern border—near Mount Hermon and the headwaters of the Jordan River (Psalm 42:6)—makes it one of the finest poems in the Bible. It's not actually clear how the psalmist, probably a Levite or one of the Temple singers, came to be so far from Jerusalem, but the deep sadness of his song suggests that he might have been among the captives led off by invading kings, perhaps even earlier than the time of the Babylonian Exile. If you've ever had a bad case of homesickness, then you know how this psalmist is feeling! His poignant longing strikes a universal cord—who hasn't experienced times when God seems absent or far away? This ardent prayer of an exiled Israelite reflects the prayer of all who long to see God and yearn for their heavenly homeland.

The imagery of the deer panting with thirst vividly expresses the unquenchable yearning experienced by the psalmist. The cry "My soul thirsts for God, / for the living God. / When shall I come and behold / the face of God?" (Psalm 42:2) vibrates with the exile's intense longing for the Lord. He is distressed by this feeling of deep thirst, which is insatiable because of the distance separating him from the Temple in Jerusalem and the hindrances of his enemies. Their mocking taunt, "Where is your God?" (42:3, 10), intensifies his pain. However, the psalmist keeps up his courage with a fervent trust in God, voiced repeatedly in the refrain "Hope in God; for I shall again praise him" (42:5, 11; 43:5), which binds the two psalms together into one poem.

The psalmist's craving to draw near to God, the fountain of living water, is inseparable from his memories of going up to the Temple sanctuary in the company of fellow worshippers (Psalm 42:4). Recalling God's past nearness, now seemingly lost, brings pain but is also the basis for hope—the psalmist will be vindicated and again "go to the altar of God" (43:4). Together, Psalms 42 and 43 offer us the assurance that our own tears, questions, disquiet, despondency, and oppression are not overlooked by the Lord. As we have known God's presence in the past, so we can trust that we will again delight in his presence in the future.

Understand!

1. Which verses illustrate the problems and conditions that the psalmist is facing in Psalm 42?

---

2. With what descriptive words does the psalmist express his pain and his need? How would you describe the psalmist's mood?

_____

_____

_____

_____

_____

3. Which phrases in Psalms 42 and 43 describe what the psalmist would like God to do for him?

_____

_____

_____

_____

_____

4. What images and attributes does the psalmist use to describe God? Why does the psalmist think God will respond to his cries? According to the psalmist himself, how will he express his gratitude when God has responded to his pleas?

_____

_____

_____

_____

_____

5. Read Psalm 13, an individual petition that has been called "a prayer in desolation." In what ways is this psalm similar to Psalm 42?

_____

_____

_____

_____

_____

▶ In the Spotlight
In the Shadow of Death

In 1534 the English Parliament passed legislation that declared King Henry VIII Supreme Head of the Church of England. Holding fast to the Catholic Church's teaching on papal authority, Sir Thomas More (b. 1478) refused to take an oath recognizing the king's supremacy, which was required by the law, and was imprisoned in the Tower of London. Fifteen months later, he was tried for treason. Convicted on perjured testimony, More was sentenced to death and beheaded on July 6, 1535. On the scaffold, he told the crowd of spectators that he was dying as "the King's good servant, but God's first."

Sir Thomas More found strength and comfort in the psalms during his imprisonment. A short version of the breviary and Psalter that he used in the tower called the *Book of Hours* still survives with marginal annotations written in his own hand. These notes give us insight into his spiritual life and inner struggles as he approached death.

More prayed the psalms frequently, and highlighted many verses in the *Book of Hours* particularly relevant to his circumstances, among them Psalm 27:3: "Though a host encamp against me, / my heart shall not fear; / though war arise against me, / yet I will be confident." Other notes reveal his awareness of his human frailty and ask for strength and the grace of virtues such as perseverance and hope—for example, he penned the word "trust" next to Psalm 23:4: "Even though I walk through the valley of the shadow of death, / I fear no evil." Next to the lines "How lovely is thy dwelling place, / O LORD of hosts! / My soul longs, yea, faints for the courts of the LORD" (Psalm 84:1-2), he wrote, "The prayer either of a man who is shut up in prison, or of one who lies sick in bed, yearning [to go] to church, or of any faithful man who yearns for heaven." And one note that reveals More's deep longing for God is especially moving when we recall that, filled with the ardent desire to see God, he wrote it while awaiting execution: "Happy the man who can say this from his soul: As a hart longs for flowing streams, / so longs my soul for thee, O God. / My soul thirsts for God, for the living God. / When shall I come and behold the face of God?" [Psalm 42:1-2].

In 1935, four hundred years after his death, St. Thomas More was canonized by Pope Pius XI. His feast day is June 22.

Grow!

1. What is your greatest desire or deepest yearning? Is your thirst for God as intense as that of the psalmist? If you feel despondent or lacking in desire for God, how might you stir up or deepen a longing for him?

_____

_____

_____

_____

_____

2. Have you ever felt "in exile," forgotten by God and far away from him? If so, why? Are there patterns or attitudes in your life that keep you distanced from God? How might you change this?

_____

_____

_____

_____

_____

3. What have you learned from the psalmist's way of praying and crying out to God in his distress? Do you feel free to express your acute pain or feelings of anguish to God? Why or why not? What do you do when you feel downcast or discouraged?

_____

_____

_____

_____

_____

4. Recall an instance when you faced severe illness, grief or other emotional pain, or false accusations. What was your prayer like then? How did you relate to God? What gave you confidence that God had heard your cry? How did you see God act and respond to your prayer in this situation?

_____

_____

_____

_____

_____

5. What role does memory play in your relationship with the Lord and in your prayer? How frequently do you spend time recalling the deeds of the Lord and your personal story of salvation and God's action in your life?

_____

_____

_____

_____

_____

▶ In the Spotlight
Deliverance through the Words
of the Psalms

For thirty long years, I tried to break the awful habit of smoking that I had begun as a teenager. Novenas, healing prayers, prayers for deliverance—nothing seemed to help for very long. Finally, one year on the feast of Mary's Assumption, I complained seriously and earnestly to God. "Lord, I can quit anytime, but I always start up again because I just can't lose the *desire* to smoke. Please, please, you have to help me!"

The very next day, the responsorial psalm at Mass nearly jumped off the page: "I need you, Lord. Come quickly to my aid. I waited, I waited for the LORD, / and he stooped toward me; he heard my cry" (Psalm 40:1). Over the next few days at Mass, the Lord spoke to me other words of hope from the psalms:

Look at me and be merciful, / for I am wretched and alone. See my hardship and my poverty. (Entrance antiphon from Psalm 25:16, 18)

Then they cried to the LORD in their need / and he rescued them from their distress. (Psalm 107:6)

Listen, Lord, and answer me. / Save your servant who trusts in you. / I call to you all day long. / Have mercy on me, Lord. (Opening verses from Psalm 86)

By the end of a week immersed in such Scripture passages, I found that I didn't care if I *ever* saw a cigarette again! I quit smoking without any difficulty.

The following February, my dear husband died. Formerly, something like this would certainly have driven me to reach for

a calming cigarette. I never even *thought* of it. Through the power of God's word, I had received real, total deliverance.
—**A great-grandmother from Ontario, Canada,** *His Word Is Among Us*

Reflect!

1. Consider your current needs or difficulties. In light of the psalmist's lament in Psalm 42, pray from your heart, telling the Lord how you feel and what you hope for. This contemporary prayer by author Joan Guntzelman may help you begin the process of expressing yourself freely to God:

> Dear God, in my distress I know that you love me and are with me. You are sheltering me, holding me close to your heart. I know that many of my struggles are simply some of the painful realities of life that everyone experiences from time to time. I also know that pouring out my heart to you is a wonderful way of letting go of my pain. Telling you all about it helps me to release my burdens to you. I trust that you will soothe my pain and comfort me. (*Turning to God in Tough Times: Prayers to Comfort the Heart and Sustain the Spirit*)

2. Reflect on the following Scripture passages that express our need and our thirst for God and the assurance that he hears our cries:

> In my distress I called upon the LORD;
>   to my God I cried for help.
> From his temple he heard my voice,
>   and my cry to him reached his ears. (Psalm 18:6)

Do not let the flood sweep over me,
　　or the deep swallow me up,
　　or the Pit close its mouth over me.

Answer me, O LORD, for your steadfast love is good;
　　according to your abundant mercy, turn to me.
Do not hide your face from your servant,
　　for I am in distress—make haste to answer me.
Draw near to me, redeem me,
　　set me free because of my enemies. (Psalm 69:15-18)

Jesus answered [the Samaritan woman at the well], "If you knew the gift of God, and who it is that is saying to you, 'Give me a drink,' you would have asked him, and he would have given you living water. . . . Those who drink of the water that I will give them will never be thirsty. The water that I will give will become in them a spring of water gushing up to eternal life." (John 4:10, 14)

The Spirit and the bride say, "Come."
And let everyone who hears say, "Come."
And let everyone who is thirsty come.
Let anyone who wishes take the water of life as a gift.
(Revelation 22:17)

▶ In the Spotlight
The Psalms, Consolation in Chaos

I am easily cast down by suffering and would be inconsolable about my sickness if I did not find in the psalms those cries of sorrow . . . which God at last answers by granting pardon and peace. During many weeks of extreme fatigue, the psalms have never been out of my hands. I have not wearied of rereading those sublime lamentations, those flights of hope, those entreaties full of love which correspond to all the wants and miseries of human nature. . . . Though the psalms were composed long ago, we still find in them the expression of our deepest anguish and the consolation of our sorrows.

—**Blessed Frederic Ozanam,** quoted in *The Saints' Guide to Learning to Pray*

The psalms can make great sense as chaotic prayer. They are full of darkness and conflict as well as joy in God's presence; they are not always pure praise but often ugly with vengeance, hatred, and smugness. In the psalms people cry out in joy and pain, bewilderment and wonder, fear, shame and rebellion; and they go on tediously telling God about their tedious lives. This is the human condition as familiar to us. The psalms are about human experience, and no part of it is hidden from God or felt to be unmentionable in his presence. They were waiting for Christ, waiting to be taken up and transformed by him, waiting to be Christified, like all human experience.

—**Maria Boulding, OSB,** *The Coming of God*

Act!

We are surrounded by many people—family members, neighbors, co-workers—who are burdened or troubled, perhaps suffering from a serious illness, grieving the death of a loved one, fighting depression, or struggling under financial difficulties.

Pray each day this week for someone you know who is in distress or need. Also ask the Lord to show you how you might help this person.

Then reach out personally and actively to that person, offering comfort and encouragement, the reassurance of God's love and care, and any practical assistance or support that you might be able to provide.

▶ In the Spotlight
Medicine for the Heart

"In the Psalter, . . . you learn about yourself. You find depicted in it all the movements of your soul, all its changes, its ups and downs, its failures and recoveries," noted the Church Father St. Athanasius. With great insight, he added, "Whatever your particular need or trouble, from this same book you can select a form of words to fit it, so that you do not merely hear and then pass on, but learn the way to remedy your ill" (*Letter to Marcellinus on the Interpretation of the Psalms*).

Here are some "prescriptions"—particular psalm verses that act as "medicine" for some common "ailments of heart":

In times of need: Psalm 17:6-7
In times of distress or loneliness: Psalm 23:1-6
When overcome with worry and anxiety: Psalm 37:3-7
In times of sadness: Psalm 43:3-5
When seeking God's forgiveness: Psalm 51:1-12
When in need of strength: Psalm 62:5-8
When God seems distant: Psalm 139:1-18
When in need of God's protection: Psalm 121:1-6
When in need of God's comfort: Psalm 103:1-14
When in need of guidance: Psalm 119:33-40
When in need of healing: Psalm 6:1-5
In times of mourning: Psalm 30:10-12

"Sit at My Right Hand"

Psalm 110:1-7

¹ The LORD says to my lord,
  "Sit at my right hand
until I make your enemies your
  footstool."

² The LORD sends out from Zion
  your mighty scepter.
  Rule in the midst of your foes.
³ Your people will offer themselves
  willingly
  on the day you lead your forces
  on the holy mountains.
From the womb of the morning,
  like dew, your youth will come to you.
⁴ The LORD has sworn and will not change his mind,
  "You are a priest forever according to the order of
  Melchizedek."

⁵ The Lord is at your right hand;
  he will shatter kings on the day of his wrath.
⁶ He will execute judgment among the nations,
  filling them with corpses;
he will shatter heads
  over the wide earth.
⁷ He will drink from the stream by the path;
  therefore he will lift up his head.

Not only a king but also a priest forever; this is the surprising promise God makes to his Anointed in this messianic psalm. God's people will be ruled by a mighty champion who will be both king and high priest.
—**Mike Aquilina and Christopher Bailey**

Many of the psalms of ancient Israel were composed to be recited by the king or as prayers, thanksgivings, or blessings for the king. Some of these "royal" or "kingship" psalms (among them, 18, 20, 21, and 45) celebrate events in the lives of Israel's kings, who were considered God's representatives on earth. (Such events might be a coronation ceremony, a ritual anointing, an enthronement ceremony, a marriage, or a victory over enemies.) Other psalms recall the promises God had made to King David—promises of an eternal dynasty and of a kingdom that would last forever. Because they were faced with the disasters and sins of the monarchy that unfolded after the reign of David, the people of Israel came to hope that these promises would be fulfilled in a "hero-king" yet to come. This anointed leader or "Messiah" (in Hebrew, *mashiah* means "anointed one") would be descended from David and would throw off the oppressor's yoke, restore the kingdom, and carry on the glorious reign of David forever. Thus, Jews and Christians alike consider those royal psalms referring to the idea of the anointing of the king as "messianic" psalms (among them, 2, 72, 89, 110, and 132).

Christians also recognize as messianic several psalms of lament—22, 31, 69, and 118. These laments have overtones of hope, victory, praise, and thanksgiving in them, as they refer to a figure that is scorned and humiliated yet ultimately vindicated, prefiguring Christ. (*Christos* is Greek for "anointed one.") Consequently, Christians recite and pray both groups of messianic psalms as prophecies about Jesus, God's anointed King and Messiah, who is also the crucified Lord, risen from the dead and seated at the right hand of the Father.

Jewish tradition interprets Psalm 110 as referring directly to the Davidic monarchy and to the Messiah-king-to-come, the son of David. Christians see in it a foreshadowing of the incarnation of Jesus Christ, true Son of God, the messianic king and eternal priest.

Originally, Psalm 110 was prayed—or delivered as an oracle by a prophet—at a new king's coronation and enthronement ceremony. Verse 1—"The LORD says to my lord, / 'Sit at my right hand'"— means that the Lord God is speaking to the king and installs the king at his right hand, a place of prestige and honor. The New Testament writers see this as referring to Jesus and quote Psalm 110 more often than any other psalm. In particular, its first verse alone is quoted or alluded to at least ten times in the New Testament (Matthew 26:64; Mark 12:35-37; 14:61-62; 16:19; Luke 20:42-43; 22:69; Acts 2:34-35; 1 Corinthians 15:25; Hebrews 1:13; 10:13).

Psalm 110 begins with the declaration that it is God who establishes the new king in his authority over his people (signified by the "mighty scepter") and brings him victory over his enemies, putting them under his feet (verses 1–2). Verse 4 speaks of the king inheriting a priestly role: "You are a priest forever according to the order of Melchizedek." Like Melchizedek, who was both priest and king of Salem at the time of Abraham (Genesis 14:18-20), the newly enthroned king of Jerusalem is also a priest. The author of the Letter to the Hebrews cites Psalm 110:4 to explain Christ's priesthood and connect it to Melchizedek (5:5-6; 7:17, 21). The psalm's prophecy is accomplished and the priesthood of Melchizedek is completed in Jesus' death, resurrection, and ascension. Moreover, as Pope Benedict XVI has noted, "The offering of bread and wine made by Melchizedek in Abraham's time" is fulfilled by Jesus, "who offers himself in the bread and in the wine and, having conquered death, brings life to all believers" (General Audience, November 16, 2011).

> Jesus Christ, true Son of God, is the messianic king and eternal priest, risen from the dead and seated at the right hand of the Father.

The final verses of Psalm 110 depict a triumphant sovereign. Supported by the Lord, who has given him power and glory, the king opposes his foes, crushing his adversaries and judging the nations. Verses 5–6 prophetically point to the Christian truth that in the ongoing battle between good and evil, Christ, our true King and Priest, prevails, victorious over Satan, sin, and evil. However, the New Testament refrains from applying the ancient mentality and gruesome imagery of verse 6 to Jesus in its literal sense: Christian theology understands that Jesus did not come to "shatter heads" and heap up "corpses" but rather to overthrow Satan so that mankind might be freed from bondage to sin and the power of darkness.

Verse 7—"He will drink from the stream by the path; / therefore he will lift up his head"—offers us an enigmatic image of the king. At a moment of respite during battle, he quenches his thirst at a stream, finding in it refreshment and fresh strength to continue on his triumphant way, holding his head high in the confidence and assurance of victory. This verse may be an allusion to a particular quasi-sacramental rite—drinking from the spring of Gihon, south of the city of Jerusalem, where the royal anointing ceremony took place (1 Kings 1:33, 38-40). It also calls to mind Gideon's army, composed of those who had lapped water from the stream before battle with the Midianites (Judges 7:5-6).

How fitting it is that we frequently pray Psalm 110 at Mass as the responsorial psalm, honoring Christ Jesus, our victorious king and merciful priest, who gives forgiveness and salvation to all people.

Understand!

1. Jesus fulfills God's promises to ancient Israel in ways that go far beyond Jewish hopes and expectations. What light does Psalm 110 shed on your own understanding of who Jesus is?

_____

_____

_____

_____

_____

_____

2. Mark 14:61-62; 16:19; 1 Corinthians 15:25; and Hebrews 1:13; 10:13 amplify the visual image and setting evoked by the opening verse of Psalm 110. What do these images convey to you about Jesus?

_____

_____

_____

_____

_____

_____

3. Why is Psalm 110's prophetic allusion to Jesus' priesthood significant? How did Jesus carry out this priestly role in his life? What are some Gospel incidents that depict Jesus in this role?

_____

_____

_____

_____

_____

_____

4. Jesus used Psalm 110 to argue that the Messiah is not just another descendant of David, but someone superior to him, of exalted and transcendent origin (Matthew 22:41-46; Mark 12:35-37). Is Jesus implying that he is the Son of God? How do you think his use of this psalm helped the early Church come to an understanding of who Jesus is and to a Christian interpretation of the psalm?

_____

_____

_____

_____

_____

_____

5. Read Psalm 72, another of the royal, messianic psalms. Pick out several verses in which you recognize messianic overtones. Name several attributes ascribed to the king in Psalm 72 that are also applicable to Jesus.

_____

_____

_____

_____

_____

_____

▶ In the Spotlight
Shedding Light on Scripture's Obscurities

Countless variations exist between the many manuscripts containing portions of Scripture that were copied by hand and passed down during more than two millennia. For example, several verses in the Hebrew manuscripts from the tenth century A.D. differ from the Greek translation of the Hebrew found in the manuscripts of the fourth century A.D. Occasionally, parts of the original texts were lost or badly corrupted. Consequently, translations into English and other vernaculars also differ in their renderings of difficult texts. Adding to the challenging task of translation is the fact that biblical Hebrew is written only with consonants. Thus, vowels, though sometimes indicated by diacritic marks, are unclear or ambiguous, so the meaning of many ancient Hebrew words can only be surmised.

Scholars recognize Psalm 110 as one of the oldest psalms. It's also considered one of the most difficult to understand. In the Septuagint, a Greek translation made in the third to second centuries B.C. of the available Hebrew texts, verse 3 reads (though somewhat obscurely) as a description of the divine sonship of the king and his origin or "begetting" from the Lord: "Yours is princely power from the day of your birth. / In holy splendor before the daystar, / like the dew I begot you" (New American Bible). This is the interpretation that the Church accepted, and this reading of Psalm 110 has had a place in Sunday Vespers in the Liturgy of the Hours from its beginning. Verse 3 has also been associated with the *lucernarium* (the ancient blessing of evening lights), referring as it does to the brightness of the daystar.

However, in some Hebrew texts, verse 3 seems to describe, also without much clarity, the "mustering" of an army and the nation's people willingly responding and gathering around their sovereign on the day of his coronation. This meaning is reflected in the New Revised Standard Version: "Your people will offer themselves willingly / on the day you lead your forces / on the holy mountains. / From the womb of the morning, / like dew, your youth will come to you."

Many uncertainties about how to best translate certain words and portions of the Hebrew Scriptures may never be resolved. Nonetheless, today's biblical scholars and experts in the study of ancient languages continue to devote their skills and energies to shedding light on Scripture's obscurities and bringing God's inspired word to us as accurately as possible.

Grow!

1. How have you experienced Jesus' kingship over your life? How does your life give concrete witness to others that Jesus is your Lord and Messiah? How do you show honor to the Lord in your life?

_____

_____

_____

_____

_____

2. What manifestations of Jesus' kingly authority do you see in the world? In what ways might God be calling you to manifest his authority over heaven and earth? Are you willing to join the "forces on the holy mountain" (Psalm 110:3) to win the battle against sin and death?

_____

_____

_____

_____

_____

3. Recall an occasion when Christ delivered you from a difficulty that was overwhelming you. Are there any "enemies"—for example, sinful habits, negative attitudes or emotions, anxieties, false accusations against you—that are currently threatening to undermine your life or relationship with the Lord? How confident are you that God can (and will!) "put these enemies under your feet"? (cf. Psalm 110:1). What might you do to grow in a deeper trust in God?

_____

_____

_____

_____

_____

_____

4. Jewish authorities were hard-hearted in their view of Jesus and refused to consider that he might truly be the Messiah because they had false assumptions about what this promised one would be like and do. Think of a time when you failed to recognize God's presence and action in your life because you were expecting something else. How did you finally become aware that the Lord was at work in those circumstances?

_____

_____

_____

_____

_____

_____

5. As Christians, we are anointed as "priest, prophet, and king" to participate in the mission of Christ in the world (*Catechism of the Catholic Church*, 1546). In what ways do you see yourself fulfilling these roles? How can you be a prophetic voice to your family, friends, and neighbors?

_____

_____

_____

_____

_____

_____

▶ In the Spotlight
Messianic Psalms of Lament

As an observant Jew, Jesus prayed the psalms throughout his life, and words from them were on his lips during his agony on the cross. His cry, "My God, my God, why have you forsaken me?" (Matthew 27:46), comes from the opening of Psalm 22, a lament that ends in profound trust in God. And with his dying breath, Jesus cried, "Father, into your hands I commend my spirit" (Luke 23:46; Psalm 31:5).

Psalms 22, 31, 69, and 118 contain many images that correspond to details that the Evangelists recorded about Jesus' passion—for example, casting lots for Jesus' garments (Psalm 22:18; Matthew 27:35) and giving vinegar to Jesus in his thirst (Psalm 69:21; John 19:29). Psalm 118 in particular helped early Jewish believers who accepted Jesus as the Messiah understand his horrific death as being part of his messianic identity and role. It serves as a link between the more purely messianic psalms about an anointed king to come, the glorious descendant of David, and psalms about a suffering figure, because it depicts one who is hard-pressed and under mortal threat but then saved by God (118:11-14, 17). As early Christians came to understand it, "The stone that the builders rejected," who is Jesus, "has become the chief cornerstone" (118:22; Matthew 21:42; Luke 20:17; Acts 4:11; 1 Peter 2:7). Thus, the Church added these psalms of lament with their descriptions of suffering, shame, reproaches, mockery, and humiliation (and, ultimately, deliverance as well) to the psalms they considered "messianic" in their prophecies about Jesus. As the Trappist monk and spiritual writer Thomas Merton wrote:

> When we recite the Psalms we must learn to recognize in them the suffering and triumphant Messias, confessing

Him with our mouth and believing in our heart that God has raised Him from the dead. Then we reap the abundant fruits of His Redemption. (*Bread in the Wilderness*)

Reflect! 3 people

1. Reflect on this observation from Blessed John Paul II:

> The Fathers [of the Church] were firmly convinced that the Psalms speak of Christ. The risen Jesus, in fact, applied the Psalms to himself when he said to the disciples: "Everything written about me in the law of Moses and the prophets and the psalms must be fulfilled" (Luke 24:44). The Fathers add that in the Psalms Christ is spoken to or it is even Christ who speaks. In saying this, they were thinking not only of the individual person of Christ, but of the *Christus totus,* the total Christ, composed of Christ the Head and his members. (General Audience, March 28, 2001)

Now read one of your favorite psalms as if it were Christ speaking to you. What difference does this make in how you pray the psalm? What might Jesus want to tell you? What might the "total Christ," the Church, be saying?

2. Read and meditate on these words of the prophet Nathan regarding King David's dynasty and the Gospel texts referring to how this is fulfilled in Jesus:

> The word of the LORD came to Nathan: Go and tell my servant David: . . . the LORD declares to you that the LORD will make you a house. When your days are fulfilled and you lie down with your ancestors, I will raise up your

offspring after you, who shall come forth from your body, and I will establish his kingdom. He shall build a house for my name, and I will establish the throne of his kingdom forever. I will be a father to him, and he shall be a son to me. . . . Your house and your kingdom shall be made sure forever before me; your throne shall be established forever. In accordance with all these words and with all this vision, Nathan spoke to David.

Then King David went in and sat before the LORD, and said, "Who am I, O Lord GOD, and what is my house, that you have brought me thus far? And yet this was a small thing in your eyes, O Lord GOD; you have spoken also of your servant's house for a great while to come. . . . And now, O Lord GOD, you are God, and your words are true, and you have promised this good thing to your servant; now therefore may it please you to bless the house of your servant, so that it may continue forever before you; for you, O Lord GOD, have spoken, and with your blessing shall the house of your servant be blessed forever." (2 Samuel 7:4-5, 11-14, 16-19, 28-29)

The angel [Gabriel] said to her, "Do not be afraid, Mary, for you have found favor with God. And now, you will conceive in your womb and bear a son, and you will name him Jesus. He will be great, and will be called the Son of the Most High, and the Lord God will give to him the throne of his ancestor David. He will reign over the house of Jacob forever, and of his kingdom there will be no end." Mary said to the angel, "How can this be, since I am a virgin?" The angel said to her, "The Holy Spirit will come upon you, and the power of the Most High will overshadow you; therefore the child to be born will be holy; he will be called Son of God. (Luke 1:30-35)

When [Jesus] came to Nazareth, where he had been brought up, he went to the synagogue on the sabbath day, as was his custom. He stood up to read, and the scroll of the prophet Isaiah was given to him. He unrolled the scroll and found the place where it was written:
"The Spirit of the Lord is upon me,
   because he has anointed me to bring good news to
      the poor.
He has sent me to proclaim release to the captives
   and recovery of sight to the blind, to let the
      oppressed go free,
to proclaim the year of the Lord's favor."
And he rolled up the scroll, gave it back to the attendant, and sat down. The eyes of all in the synagogue were fixed on him. Then he began to say to them, "Today this scripture has been fulfilled in your hearing." (Luke 4:16-21; see also Isaiah 61:1-2)

▶ In the Spotlight
Vengeance and Curses in the Psalms

How do Christians pray psalms that contain vindictive curses and call for God to take vengeance on the enemies of the psalmists? At least thirty such outbursts are included in the Book of Psalms. Here are just a few:

He will repay my enemies for their evil. / In your faithfulness, put an end to them. (Psalm 54:5)

Let death come upon them; / let them go down alive to Sheol. (Psalm 55:15)

So repay them for their crime; / in wrath cast down the peoples, O God! (Psalm 56:7)

Let them be blotted out of the book of the living; / let them not be enrolled among the righteous. (Psalm 69:28)

Such verses, called "imprecatory prayer," "vent the rage of saints who recognize that vengeance is exclusively God's territory, but who at the same time feel the injustices of this world very deeply and who desperately want God to correct the inequities that always seem to leave the righteous/weak at the mercy (or mercilessness) of the wicked/powerful," according to Scripture scholar Kevin J. Youngblood. "Throughout church history Christians have wrestled with the tension created by the presence of such prayers alongside Jesus' ethic of love and forgiveness."

As Christians, however, our true "enemies" are sin and death. We can read these prayers with that idea in mind, recognizing that we are all involved in a spiritual battle against evil. We can also feel the same outrage as the psalmist at the evil that we see, even while retaining an attitude of forgiveness. Finally, these prayers help us to release our desire for vengeance to God. We can trust in God's justice. This frees us from the need to take revenge ourselves, and allows us instead to be merciful to our enemies.

Act!

Exercise your trust in Jesus the Messiah and his power to transform you. Look back at question 3 in the Grow! section on page 104. In light of your reflections on "enemies," ask the Lord to "rescue" you. During the coming week, bring your needs before the Lord in prayer each day. Then cooperate with his work in you. Don't forget to thank him for his saving action.

▶ In the Spotlight
David's Enduring Throne

Counted among the royal and messianic psalms, Psalm 89 joyously celebrates the unconditional promise that God made to establish King David's dynasty. Although David and his descendants failed to keep God's commands and were to be justly punished as a consequence (Psalm 89:31-33), God nevertheless declared,

> I will not violate my covenant,
>   or alter the word that went forth from my lips.
> Once and for all I have sworn by my holiness;
>   I will not lie to David.
> His line shall continue forever,
>   and his throne endure before me like the sun. (89:34-36)

However, in events that seemed to belie God's word, Israel fell into disgrace at the hands of a foreign nation. Her king was brought down, and it appeared that David's line had been cut off (Psalm 89:38-45). How could Israel reconcile this destruction with God's promises? The situation required that God's promise to David be understood in a new sense—as a description of an ideal king who would one day inherit David's throne.

Psalm 89 ends with a great cry wrenched from the heart of a disappointed yet hopeful people (89:46-52). In anguish the psalmist implores God to remember his promise and restore his people by sending a righteous king to reign over them again: "Lord, where is your steadfast love of old, / which by your faithfulness you swore to David?" (89:49).

The people of Israel were mistaken in their understanding and expectation of a political ruler, yet their faith would finally be vindicated. God would answer their pleas, not by restoring the ancient monarchy, but by raising up, in the words of one hymn writer, "great David's greater son." Ultimately, Jesus Christ, a descendant of David, would rule over all as King, Savior, and Messiah.

Practical Pointers for Bible Discussion Groups

A Bible discussion group is another key that can help us unlock God's word. Participating in a discussion or study group—whether through a parish, a prayer group, or a neighborhood—offers us the opportunity to grow not only in our love for God's word but also in our love for one another. We don't have to be trained Scripture scholars to benefit from discussing and studying the Bible together. Bible study groups provide environments in which we can worship and pray together and strengthen our relationships with other Christians. The following guidelines can help a group get started and run smoothly.

Getting Started

- Decide on a regular time and place to meet. Meeting on a regular basis allows the group to maintain continuity without losing momentum from the previous discussion.

- Set a time limit for each session. An hour and a half is a reasonable length of time in which to have a rewarding discussion on the material contained in each of the sessions in this guide. However, the group may find that a longer time is even more advantageous. If it is necessary to limit the meeting to an hour, select sections of the material that are of greatest interest to the group.

- Designate a moderator or facilitator to lead the discussions and keep the meetings on schedule. This person's role is to help preserve good group dynamics by keeping the discussion on track. He or she should help ensure that no one monopolizes the session and that each person—including the shyest or quietest individual—is offered an opportunity to speak. The group may want to ask members to take turns moderating the sessions.

- Provide enough copies of the study guide for each member of the group, and ask everyone to bring a Bible to the meetings. Each session's Scripture text and related passages for reflection are printed in full in the guides, but you will find that a Bible is helpful for looking up other passages and cross-references. The translation provided in this guide is the New Revised Standard Version (Catholic Edition). You may also want to refer to other translations—for example, the New American Bible or the New Jerusalem Bible—to gain additional insights into the text.

- Try to stay faithful to your commitment and attend as many sessions as possible. Not only does regular participation provide coherence and consistency to the group discussions, but it also demonstrates that members value one another and are committed to sharing their lives with one another.

Session Dynamics

- Read the material for each session in advance and take time to consider the questions and your answers to them. The single most important key to any successful Bible study is having everyone prepared to participate.

- As a courtesy to all members of your group, try to begin and end each session on schedule. Being prompt respects the other commitments of the members and allows enough time for discussion. If the group still has more to discuss at the end of the allotted time, consider continuing the discussion at the next meeting.

- Open the sessions with prayer. A different person could have the responsibility of leading the opening prayer at each session. The prayer could be a spontaneous one, a traditional prayer such as the Our Father, or one that relates to the topic of that particular meeting. The members of the group might also want to begin some of the meetings with a song or hymn. Whatever you choose, ask the Holy Spirit to guide your discussion and study of the Scripture text presented in that session.

- Contribute actively to the discussion. Let the members of the group get to know you, but try to stick to the topic so that you won't divert the discussion from its purpose. And resist the temptation to monopolize the conversation, so that everyone will have an opportunity to learn from one another.

- Listen attentively to everyone in the group. Show respect for the other members and their contributions. Encourage, support, and affirm them as they share. Remember that many questions have more than one answer and that the experience of everyone in the group can be enriched by considering a variety of viewpoints.

- If you disagree with someone's observation or answer to a question, do so gently and respectfully, in a way that shows that you value the person who made the comment, and then explain your own point of view. For example, rather than saying, "You're wrong!" or "That's ridiculous!" try something like "I think I see what you're getting at, but I think that Jesus was saying something different in this passage." Be careful to avoid sounding aggressive or argumentative. Then watch to see how the subsequent discussion unfolds. Who knows? You may come away with a new and deeper perspective.

- Don't be afraid of pauses and reflective moments of silence during the session. People may need some time to think about a question before putting their thoughts into words.

- Maintain and respect confidentiality within the group. Safeguard the privacy and dignity of each member by not repeating what has been shared during the discussion session unless you have been given permission to do so. That way everyone will get the greatest benefit out of the group by feeling comfortable enough to share on a deep and personal level.

- End the session with prayer. Thank God for what you have learned through the discussion, and ask him to help you integrate it into your life.

The Lord blesses all our efforts to come closer to him. As you spend time preparing for and meeting with your small group, be confident in the knowledge that Christ will fill you with wisdom, insight, and grace and the ability to see him at work in your daily life.

Sources and Acknowledgments

Introduction

Augustine, *Confessions,* Book IX (modern adaptation).

Benedict XVI, General Audience, June 22, 2011, http://www.vatican.va/holy_father/benedict_xvi/audiences/2011/ documents/hf_ben-xvi_aud_20110622_en.html.

Thomas Merton, *Bread in the Wilderness* (New York: New Directions Publishing Corporation, 1997), 47–48.

Session 1: Wisdom Psalms

Pius X, Apostolic Constitution, *Divino Afflatu,* quoted in *The Liturgy of the Hours,* vol. IV (New York: Catholic Book Publishing Co., 1975), 1336.

M. Basil Pennington, OCSO, *Psalms: A Spiritual Commentary* (Woodstock, VT: Skylight Paths Publishing, 2008), 5.

R.A.F. MacKenzie, SJ, *Old Testament Reading Guide: The Book of Psalms—A Selection* (Collegeville, MN: The Liturgical Press, 1967), 110.

Nahum M. Sarna, *Songs of the Heart: An Introduction to the Book of Psalms* (New York: Schoken Books, 1993), 5.

Ben Patterson, *God's Prayer Book: The Power and Pleasure of Praying the Psalms* (Carol Stream, IL: Tyndale House Publishers, Inc., 2008), 21.

Athanasius of Alexandria, *Letter to Marcellinus on the Interpretation of the Psalms*, http://www.athanasius.com/psalms/aletterm.htm.

Bernard of Clairvaux, *Talks on the Song of Songs,* ed. and modernized by Bernard Bangley (Brewster, MA: Paraclete Press, 2002), 13.

Session 2: Psalms of Praise

M. Basil Pennington, OSCO, *Psalms: A Spiritual Commentary* (Woodstock, VT: Skylight Paths Publishing, 2008), 123.

John V. Sheridan, *Living the Psalms: Selections from the Psalms with Meditations* (Boston: Pauline Books & Media, 1996), 258.

Jean-Pierre Prévost, "Sing, O Sing Praises to Our God," *God's Word Today*, July 2009, 42.

Victor-Antoine d'Avila-Latourrette, *Blessings of the Daily: A Monastic Book of Days* (Liguori, MO: Liguori, 2002), 266.

Ambrose, *Explanation of the Psalms*, quoted in *The Liturgy of the Hours,* vol. III (New York: Catholic Book Publishing Co., 1975), 348.

Marie of the Incarnation, quoted in Louise Perrotta, *The Saints' Guide to Learning to Pray* (Ann Arbor, MI: Servant Publications, 2001), 69–70.

Francis of Assisi, "The Praises of God," http://francis-bible.org/writings/witings_francis_prayers.html.

Session 3: Psalms of Repentance

Augustine, quoted in Paul Thigpen, *A Dictionary of Quotes from the Saints* (Ann Arbor, MI: Servant Publications, 2001), 43.

Benedict XVI, *Jesus of Nazareth—Holy Week: From the Entrance into Jerusalem to the Resurrection* (San Francisco: Ignatius Press, 2011), 74.

Victor-Antoine d'Avila-Latourrette, *Blessings of the Daily: A Monastic Book of Days* (Liguori, MO: Liguori, 2002), 284–285.

Woodeene Koenig-Bricker, *Asking God for the Gifts He Wants to Give You* (Frederick, MD: The Word Among Us Press, 2008), 47–48.

John Vianney, quoted in *A Dictionary of Quotes from the Saints*, 44.

George Martin, "Repentance and Forgiveness," *God's Word Today,* March 1981, 30.

Session 4: Psalms of Thanksgiving

John Cassian, quoted in Rosemary Ellen Guiley, *The Quotable Saint* (New York, NY: Checkmark Books, 2002), 274.

Benedict XVI, General Audience, December 7, 2005, http://www.vatican.va/holy_father/benedict_xvi/audiences/2005/documents/hf_ben-xvi_aud_20051207_en.html.

Hannah Whitall Smith, *Daily He Leads Me: Inspirational Devotions for Every Day of the Year* (Ann Arbor, MI: Servant Publications, 1985), 157.

Session 5: Psalms of Lament and Entreaty

John V. Sheridan, *Living the Psalms: Selections from the Psalms with Meditations* (Boston: Pauline Books & Media, 1996), 181.

Thomas More's Prayer Book, quoted in James Monti, *The King's Good Servant But God's First: The Life and Writings of St. Thomas More* (San Francisco: Ignatius Press, 1997), 354–357.

A great-grandmother from Ontario, Canada, adapted from Louise Perotta, *His Word Is Among Us: Personal Encounters with God in Scripture* (Frederick, MD: The Word Among Us Press, 2004), 26–28.

Joan Guntzelman, *Turning to God in Tough Times: Prayers to Comfort the Heart and Sustain the Spirit* (Frederick, MD: The Word Among Us Press, 2011), 66.

Frederic Ozanam, quoted in Louise Perrotta, *The Saints' Guide to Learning to Pray* (Ann Arbor, MI: Servant Publications, 2001), 70.

Maria Boulding, OSB, *The Coming of God* (Conception, MO: The Printery House, 2000), 101.

Athanasius of Alexandria, *Letter to Marcellinus on the Interpretation of the Psalms,* http://www.athanasius.com/psalms/aletterm.htm.

Session 6: Royal and Messianic Psalms

Mike Aquilina and Christopher Bailey, *Praying the Psalms with the Early Christians: Ancient Songs for Modern Hearts* (Frederick, MD: The Word Among Us Press, 2009), 148.

Benedict XVI, General Audience, November 16, 2011, http://www
.vatican.va/holy_father/benedict_xvi/audiences/2011/documents/
hf_ben-xvi_aud_20111116_en.html.

Thomas Merton, *Bread in the Wilderness* (New York: New
Directions Publishing Corporation, 1997), 70.

John Paul II, General Audience, March 28, 2001,
http://www.vatican.va/holy_father/john_paul_ii/audiences/2001/
documents/hf_jp-ii_aud_20010328_en.html.

Kevin J. Youngblood, "Don't Get Even, Get Mad! Imprecatory
Prayer as a Neglected Spiritual Discipline (Psalm 69)," *Leaven* 19,
Issue 3 (2012), http://digitalcommons.pepperdine.edu/leaven/vol19/
iss3/8.

Also in The Word Among Us

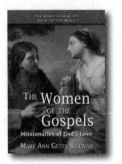

The Women of the Gospels: Missionaries of God's Love
Item# BTWFE9

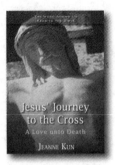

Jesus' Journey to the Cross: A Love unto Death
Item# BTWGE9

Treasures Uncovered: The Parables of Jesus
Item# BTWAE5

Mighty in Power: The Miracles of Jesus
Item# BTWBE6

Food from Heaven: The Eucharist in Scripture
Item# BTWCE7

Six Sessions for Individuals or Groups

Keys to the Bible Series

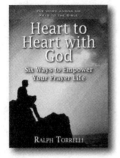

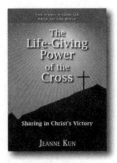

Heart to Heart with God: Six Ways to Empower Your Prayer Life
Item# BTWEE8

Moved by the Spirit: God's Power at Work in His People
Item# BTWDE8

The Life-Giving Power of the Cross: Sharing in Christ's Victory
Item# BTWKE2

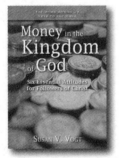

Money in the Kingdom of God: Six Essential Attitudes for Followers of Christ
Item# BTWHE0

Embracing God's Plan for Marriage: A Scripture Study for Couples
Item# BTWHE0

Each of the Keys to the Bible study sessions features

- the full Scripture text;
- a short commentary;
- questions for reflection, discussion, and personal application;
- "In the Spotlight" sections featuring wisdom from the saints and the Church, root meanings of Greek words, fascinating historical background, and stories of faith from contemporary people.

To order call 1-800-775-9673 or order online at wau.org

the WORD among us®

The *Spirit* of Catholic Living

This book was published by The Word Among Us. Since 1981, The Word Among Us has been answering the call of the Second Vatican Council to help Catholic laypeople encounter Christ in the Scriptures.

The name of our company comes from the prologue to the Gospel of John and reflects the vision and purpose of all of our publications: to be an instrument of the Spirit, whose desire is to manifest Jesus' presence in and to the children of God. In this way, we hope to contribute to the Church's ongoing mission of proclaiming the gospel to the world so that all people would know the love and mercy of our Lord and grow ever more deeply in love with him.

Our monthly devotional magazine, *The Word Among Us*, features meditations on the daily and Sunday Mass readings, and currently reaches more than one million Catholics in North America and another half million Catholics in one hundred countries around the world. Our book division, The Word Among Us Press, publishes numerous books, Bible studies, and pamphlets that help Catholics grow in their faith.

To learn more about who we are and what we publish, log on to our website at www.wau.org. There you will find a variety of Catholic resources that will help you grow in your faith.

Embrace His Word, Listen to God . . .

www.wau.org